D0297211

VIKINGS

A Dark History of the Norse People

VIKINGS

A Dark History of the Norse People

MARTIN J. DOUGHERTY

NEW HOLLAND

First published by New Holland Publishers in 2014
• London • Sydney • Auckland

The Chandlery Unit 114 50 Westminster Bridge Road London SE1 7QY United Kingdom
1/66 Gibbes Street Chatswood NSW 2067 Australia
218 Lake Road Northcote Auckland New Zealand

All rights reserved. No part of this publication may be reproduced, stored in a retrieval system, or transmitted in any form or by any means, electronic, mechanical, photocopying, recording, or otherwise, without prior written permission of the copyright holder.

A record of this book is held at the British Library and the National Library of Australia.

ISBN: 9781742575971

Copyright © 2013 Amber Books Ltd

Published by Amber Books Ltd
74–77 White Lion Street London N1 9PF United Kingdom
www.amberbooks.co.uk

Project Editor: Sarah Uttridge
Designer: Jerry Williams
Picture Research: Terry Forshaw

10 9 8 7 6 5 4 3 2 1

Printed in China by Toppan Leefung Printing Limited

Keep up with New Holland Publishers on Facebook
www.facebook.com/NewHollandPublishers

Picture Credits

Alamy: 8 top (Dough Houghton), 12 (Jon Arnold Images), 14 both (Prisma Archivo), 15 (Art Archive), 18 (Latitude Stock), 34 bottom (Art Gallery Collection), 36 (World History Archive), 48 (Image Broker), 50 (Simon Tranter Photography), 52 (Interfoto), 53 (Sindre Ellingsen), 64 (Ladi Kirn), 69 (Classic Image), 71 (David Lyons), 74 (Colouria Media), 79 top (David Muenker), 80 (All Canada Photos), 81 (Cindy Hopkins), 90 (Chris Hellier), 91 (Interfoto), 103 (Montagu Images), 112 (North Wind), 114 (Holmes Garden Photos), 132 (Choups), 138 (Mary Evans Picture Library), 141 (Robert Harding Picture Library), 154 (National Geographic), 158 (Art Archive), 163 (Photo 12), 164 (Phil Degginger), 165 (John Robertson), 166 bottom (TPM Photostock), 167 (North Wind), 168 (Les Gibbon), 185 (North Wind), 189 (Rolf Hicker Photography), 190 (Earthscapes/Tony Wright), 191 (19th Era), 200 (Art Gallery Collection), 202 bottom (Florilegius), 203 (Glenn Harper), 205 (Les Polders), 208 (Print Collector), 212 (Hilary Morgan), 220 (North Wind), 221 top (IsKa)

Amber Books: 157

Bridgeman Art Library: 149 (Biblioteques des Arts Decoratifs/Archives Charmet), 207 (Stapleton Collection)

Corbis: 6 (The Print Collector), 7 top (Bo Zaunders), 11 (Ted Spiegel), 17 (Werner Forman), 20 (Bettmann), 32 (Werner Forman), 40 (National Geographic Vintage), 41 top (Werner Forman), 47 (Werner Forman), 49 (Heritage Images), 70 (Blue Lantern Studio), 93 (National Geographic Society), 106 (Stefano Bianchetti), 108 (Bettmann), 110 (Arctic Images), 123 top (Heritage Images), 124 both (Ted Spiegel), 130 (Werner Forman), 145 bottom (Bettmann), 152 (Ted Spiegel), 153 top (Werner Forman)

Dorling Kindersley: 66 (Tony Smith), 77 (Liz McAulay), 78, 84 (Frank Greenaway), 85 top (Peter Anderson), 113 both (Gary Ombler), 117 both (Andy Crawford), 118-119 both (Gary Ombler), 125-128 all (Gary Ombler), 131, 133 bottom (David Leffman), 134 (Dave King), 160

Dreamstime: 8 bottom (Markus Gann), 13 (Markus Gann), 19 (Klavlav4ik), 25 (Ekaterina Frebus), 26 (Markus Gann), 27 bottom (Oleg Doroshin), 28 (Patrimonio Designs), 34 top (Jaroslaw Grudzinski), 37 (Andrey Kuzmin), 41 bottom (Klavlav4ik), 42 (Markus Gann), 43 (Giovanni Gagliardi), 45 (Doroo), 55 (Tt), 56 (Andrew Burgess), 58 (Ky Talpa), 59 (Frank Bach), 67 (Ky Talpa), 72 (Jaroslaw Grudzinski), 75 (Markus Gann), 87 (Kris Gun 01), 89 (Doroo), 92 (Andrew Burgess), 97 (Muscat Christian), 99 (Markus Gann), 101 (Tim@Awe), 102 (Markus Gann), 111 (Aleksey Solodov), 120 (Creativefire), 122 top (Markus Gann), 123 bottom (Klavlav4ik), 133 top (Markus Gann), 135 (Oleg Doroshin), 145 top (Jaroslaw Grudzinski), 147 (Kris Gun 01), 155 (Tt), 159 bottom (Oleg Doroshin), 162 (Markus Gann), 166 top (Ekaterina Frebus), 169 (Markus Gann), 170 (Ky Talpa), 176 (Harald), 177 (Tt), 186 (Markus Gann), 199 (Klavlav4ik), 202 top (Ekaterina Frebus), 209 (Markus Gann), 213 (Tt), 216 (Markus Gann), 218 (Adres Lebedev), 219 (Ekaterina Frebus), 221 bottom (Andrew Burgess)

Arni Ein: 140 (Published under Creative Commons Attribution-Share Alike 3.0 Unported License)

Mary Evans Picture Library: 22 (Arthur Rackham), 24, 27 top (Interfoto/Sammalung Rauch), 29, 30 (IBL Bildbyra), 31, 33, 35, 44, 46, 60, 61 (Interfoto/Sammalung Rauch), 73, 142, 144 (Edwin Mullan Collection), 172, 175, 178 (Interforo Agentur), 180 (Douglas McCarthy), 182 (Edwin Mullan Collection), 184, 194, 196 (Iberfoto/M. C. Esteban), 204 (Edwin Mullan Collection), 206, 210

FLPA: 83 (Tui de Roy), 188 (Image Broker)

Fotolia: 76, 104 & 192 all (Michael Boiero)

Getty Images: 9 (Werner Forman), 39 (De Agostini), 57 (Bridgeman Art Library), 63 (De Agostini), 65 (Universal Images Group), 72 (Universal Images Group), 82 (Time & Life Pictures), 88 (Superstock), 95 (British Library/Robana), 107 (Universal Images Group), 122 bottom (Jeff J. Mitchell), 129 top (Universal Images Group/Werner Forman), 129 bottom (Bridgeman Art Library/Hans Dahl), 136 (Universal Images Group), 148 (Minden Pictures/Jim Brandenburg), 150 (Jim Brandenburg/Minden Pictures), 159 bottom (Bridgeman Art Library/Jacobo Robusti Tintoretto), 161 (Universal Images Group), 171 (National Geographic/Michael Hampshire), 179 (British Library/Robana), 183 (Time & Life Pictures/Marvin Lichtner), 187 (National Geographic/Peter V. Bianchi), 193 (Time & Life Pictures), 197 (Leemage), 215 (Popperfoto)

Istockphoto: 7 bottom (Denise Kappa), 23 & 139 (Evgeny Sergeev), 151 (Denise Kappa)

Photos.com: 137, 217

Shutterstock: 62 (RH Images), 68 (Route 66), 79 bottom (Roman Kaplanski), 85 bottom (RH Images), 86 (David Persson), 109 (Route 66), 115 (Roman Kaplanski), 116 (RH Images), 153 bottom (Route 66), 174 (RH Images) 201 (Roman Kaplanski)

TopFoto: 38 (Charles Walker Collection), 96 (HIP/Museum of London), 121 (Granger Collection), 156 (Granger Collection)

INTRODUCTION

Few peoples or groups have ever exerted such an influence on popular culture as the Vikings. They have given us everything from the foundation of modern cities to comic-book superheroes. Their explorations and raids put islands and even continents on the map. Their depredations are, of course, legendary.

And yet most of what has passed into popular culture about the Vikings is just that: legend. For the Vikings, at least as they are popularly depicted – sea-raiders in horned helmets, drinking mead from skull goblets and longing to die gloriously in battle – never actually existed.

Even the famous 'quote' – 'From the fury of the Northmen, Good Lord, deliver us' – is quite possibly a myth. It has been attributed to many religious figures of the time, and it is certain that many people prayed for exactly that. But the true original source is hard to find; there may not even be one. It may be that the most common quote associated with the Vikings, the phrase that more than anything else sums up their deeds, is itself a modern invention.

The reality of the people who have become known as the Vikings is rather more complex than the popular version; at once far more mundane and in many ways even more incredible than the well-known tales of bloodthirsty raiders and grim warriors. These were the people who voyaged across the hostile North Atlantic Ocean in open-topped ships, who carried their vessels overland to reach the Russian rivers, and sailed down them to find new trade partners

BELOW: More than anything else, the longship is a symbol of the Vikings. In these small but seaworthy vessels they fought, raided, traded and pushed back the boundaries of the known world.

LEFT: Much of what we know about the Vikings comes from burial sites like this one at Aalborg in Denmark. Finds must be correctly interpreted if they are to increase our understanding of the Viking culture.

or sources of plunder. They were explorers, settlers and traders as well as warriors, and their legacy helped shape the modern world.

The Historical Evidence

What we know about the Vikings comes from many sources, none of them completely reliable. Conventional archaeology has unearthed artefacts, burial sites and settlements, allowing us to study what the Vikings left behind – but only the relatively small amount of material that is well preserved. We can make inferences and take educated guesses as to the significance or even function of an item, but we cannot be certain. Some known 'facts' are extrapolated from relatively obscure sources, such as the imprint of long-decayed cloth on jewellery found in a grave. Although highly intelligent experts made these extrapolations, they can never be more than a best guess.

Experimental archaeology has allowed us to learn about how the Vikings built their homes and ships, and how they fought. While some re-enactors do no more than play at being 'movie Vikings', many are dedicated researchers who have done good work in reconstructing what might have been. In terms of fighting with an axe or building a ship, chances are that a person working under similar conditions with the same materials and tools will take a similar approach whatever century he is from.

RIGHT: To some, Viking re-enactments are a fun game of make-believe. To others they are an opportunity for hands-on research into every aspect of the Viking way of life.

We can also learn a lot from historical writings, but these are inevitably biased. We owe much of what was written about the Vikings to Churchmen or the inhabitants of kingdoms that had felt the fury of the Norsemen. Even without intentional bias, their viewpoint would be coloured by the fact that they themselves were not Vikings and did not understand the Viking psyche or way of life. In many cases they were writing from observation of only one segment of Viking society – usually warriors, raiders or trading parties whose behaviour in foreign lands might be quite different to their home life.

One of the most 'direct' sources on the Vikings is the body of poetry and oral history that forms the sagas. However, these are heroic tales told over and over for years until they were finally written down centuries after the events they depict. In many cases the events of a saga can be tied to historical evidence or corroborated by other means, but ultimately the sagas are fictionalized adventures that may be no more accurate than the average historical novel.

When taken all together, these sources allow us to build a picture of who the Vikings were and what they did – and, more importantly, why. The popular image of wanton destruction and carnage perpetrated by mobs of hairy, filthy men is not in all ways unwarranted. The Vikings did pillage and they did destroy places of value and beauty. Their raids brought misery to their victims and turmoil to many regions. They also offended people who were in a position to write history and have it remembered.

The Christian Church feared and hated the Vikings for their destruction of monasteries; prominent clerics made sure that the deeds of the raiders were recorded and made known. Their outrage was justified and understandable, but it was only one side of the story. The Vikings, in short, have had a lot of bad press as a result of their choice of targets, and for years much of what was 'known' about them was based on what amounts to hostile propaganda.

It is true that the Vikings were a violent people. Strength and fighting ability were vital to the survival of the trader or explorer, and a man had to defend his home, family and community from those who would take all he had.

The Vikings' actions made sense from their perspective, and while there were undoubtedly some among them who enjoyed destruction for its own sake, there were economic, political and social reasons for what they did. They were not murderous lunatics, killing anyone in their path. There was a logic to their raids and to their settlement patterns. Their gains were at the expense of others, but that was the way of the world at the time. The strong took from the weak, and fortune favoured the brave.

Word-fame

The Vikings were certainly strong, and they were brave. Theirs was a culture that valued 'word-fame' above all else. They believed that a man could earn a sort of immortality if his deeds were remembered and talked of among the living. A short but remarkable life was better than decades of mediocrity. Word-fame was won by bravery in battle, spectacular feats of seamanship, victory in manly contests of strength or skill, and so forth. The 'fury' of the Vikings was, to a great extent, fuelled by peer pressure, with warriors not wanting to be outdone by their comrades. Small wonder, then, that these people ranged

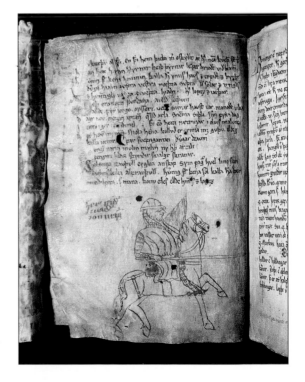

BELOW: Much of the 'first-hand' information we have on the Vikings comes from the sagas, which were passed down as oral traditions for generations before finally being written down.

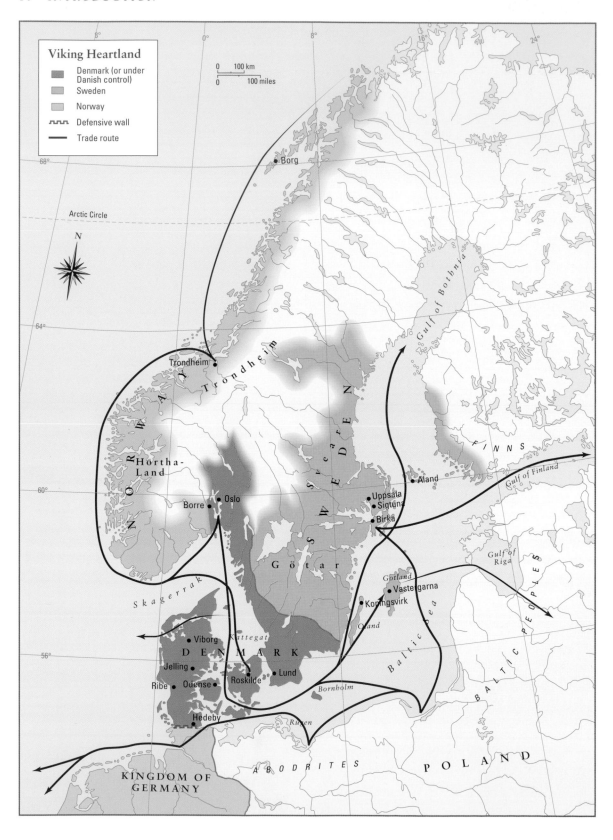

Viking Heartland

Denmark (or under Danish control)

Sweden

Norway

Defensive wall

Trade route

0 100 km
0 100 miles

N

Borg

Arctic Circle

Gulf of Bothnia

Trondheim • Trondheim

Trondheim

N O R W A Y

S V E A F E N

F I N N S

Hortha-Land

Åland

Gulf of Finland

Borre • Oslo

Uppsala
Sigtuna
Birka

G ö t a r

Gulf of Riga

Götland
• Vastergarna
• Koningsvirk

Öland

Baltic Sea

B A L T I C   P E O P L E S

Skagerrak

• Viborg

Kattegat

D E N M A R K

Jelling •

Roskilde • • Lund

Ribe • Odense •

Bornholm

Hedeby

Rügen

A B O D R I T E S

P O L A N D

KINGDOM OF
GERMANY

all over the known world and extended its boundaries. They took what they wanted when an opportunity presented itself, and they had little regard for those weaker than them.

The Viking Age

The Vikings belong to a very precise period in history. The Viking Age, as recognized by historians, began with a bloody raid on Lindisfarne in 793 AD, and ended at Hastings in 1066. In the intervening 300 years or so, Viking culture changed significantly. More importantly, perhaps, the changes wrought by the Vikings were enormous; the sheer extent of their influence on later societies is hard to comprehend.

To fully understand the effects that the Vikings had on history, and the effects that they are still having today, it is necessary to examine their deeds and their culture, to understand who they were and where they came from. Theirs is not a simple tale. It has rung down the ages to create a legend that might have become distorted, but which remains one of the great stories of all history.

Those first Vikings, arriving on Lindisfarne in 793 AD, would have been pleased with the degree of word-fame they were about to earn. They are long dead, their plunder spent and their very society gone from the Earth, but their deeds are still recounted in the twenty-first century. Few men have ever achieved more.

OPPOSITE: The people now commonly referred to as Vikings originated in Denmark, Sweden and Norway, spreading their culture to other regions by settlement and integration.

LEFT: This carving at Lindisfarne represents a band of armed raiders, which was all most people saw of the complex Viking society.

1

ORIGINS OF THE VIKINGS

History became aware of the people who are today referred to as Vikings in 793 AD, when a force of raiders from across the North Sea landed on Lindisfarne Island and sacked the monastery there. This was no chance landfall, nor was it the first time that Viking ships had landed on the Northumbrian coast.

The raiders knew about the monastery and the easy plunder to be had there from their previous expeditions. The origin of these raiders is open to some debate. Most historians agree that they were Scandinavians, although it has been suggested that they might have been Frisians. It is most likely that they were of Danish or Norwegian origin, possibly sailing from settlements in the Orkney or Shetland Islands. Contemporary sources refer to them as coming 'from the north' or 'from the land of robbers', which suggests that enough raids had occurred previously for these seafarers to have acquired a reputation long before they struck Lindisfarne.

OPPOSITE: **The threat of further Viking raids caused the monks to abandon Lindisfarne. It was not until around 1150 AD, after the end of the Viking Era, that the site was reoccupied and Lindisfarne Priory was built.**

RIGHT: These greenstone tools date from 7500 to 5500 BC, a time when Jutland and the Danish Islands were sparsely populated by small farming communities.

BELOW: Flint daggers of this sort began to be replaced by bronze around 1700 BC. Bronze use was at first limited, but its clear advantages over stone tools led to a rapid expansion of metalworking in Scandinavia.

The sacking of Lindisfarne was a dramatic event, and is now seen as the emergence onto the stage of a new and frightening people. It is a simple and clear-cut starting point for the Viking Age, but the men of the north did not simply wake up one morning and decide to ravage the coasts of Europe for the next 300 years. So why did they do so? Where did they come from and what drove them to such brutality?

Early Habitation

Humans may have inhabited Scandinavia more than 200,000 years ago, before the last Ice Age. Any human population of that era was driven out or killed off by climatic conditions, and it was not until 8000–9000 BC that humans returned to the area. There is evidence of Old Stone Age habitation in Denmark during the period 8000–4000 BC, such as stone carvings.

Farming and livestock herding allowed a more settled lifestyle during the New Stone Age (4000–1500 BC) and numerous settlements from this era have been discovered. The introduction of bronze tools around 2000–1500 BC allowed improved farming and industrial techniques that could support a larger population – and of course made conflict between rival groups more deadly.

In the Bronze Age, society in Scandinavia was based around small communities with some individuals being rich enough to afford lavish burials surrounded by bronze tools and weapons. Many of these weapons show signs of hard use, suggesting that conflict was commonplace. Trade was also widespread, with some areas of Scandinavia importing large quantities of metal for use by local craftsmen.

The Iron Age

The climate in Bronze Age Scandinavia was warmer than it is today, although a cooling that occurred around 500 BC may have made life much harder for the people of the region. At around the same time the use of iron became far more prevalent. At first it was used mainly by bronzesmiths to make their bronze-working tools but eventually a move to iron tools and weapons took place. This made the large-scale importation of metals less necessary, as iron was available locally and in abundance.

BELOW: **Ironworking was an important innovation in Scandinavia.** Not only could better weapons be produced, but the need to import materials was reduced as Scandinavia had large iron deposits.

Although the Roman Empire never reached into Scandinavia, the people of the region traded with Roman territories and undoubtedly absorbed elements of Roman culture and technology. Roman writings of the period show a vague familiarity with Scandinavian names and some concepts that might have been derived from Scandinavian culture, although some of these sources speak of men with the heads of dogs or vultures, so their accuracy in other areas is debatable.

Archaeological finds suggest that the Scandinavians of the Iron Age launched seaborne raids, sometimes in significant numbers, and that they built hillforts and other defences. Perhaps these were constructed for protection from the raids of other groups. Technology, particularly metalsmithing, made advances during this period. Intricate designs of gold became quite common, especially as the Roman Empire declined and ceased actively

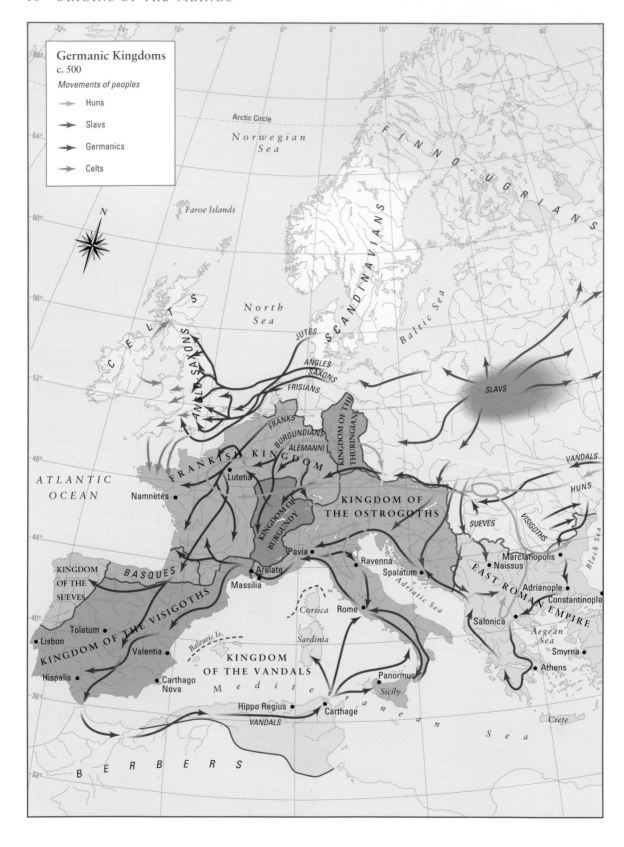

Germanic Kingdoms
c. 500
Movements of peoples

Huns
Slavs
Germanics
Celts

N

Arctic Circle

Norwegian Sea

SCANDINAVIANS

FINNO-UGRIANS

Faroe Islands

North Sea

Baltic Sea

CELTS

JUTES

SLAVS

ANGLES
SAXONS

FRISIANS

ANGLO-SAXONS

FRANKS
BURGUNDIANS
ALEMANNI

KINGDOM OF THE THURINGIANS

VANDALS

ATLANTIC OCEAN

FRANKISH KINGDOM

Lutetia

HUNS

Namnetes

KINGDOM OF BURGUNDY

KINGDOM OF THE OSTROGOTHS

SUEVES

VISIGOTHS

Pavia

Ravenna

Marcianopolis
Naissus

EAST ROMAN EMPIRE

KINGDOM OF THE SUEVES

BASQUES

Arelate
Massilia

Spalatum

Adrianople

Black Sea

Constantinople

Toletum

KINGDOM OF THE VISIGOTHS

Corsica

Rome

Salonica

Adriatic Sea

Lisbon

Valentia

Balearic Is.

Sardinia

KINGDOM OF THE VANDALS

Panormus

Aegean Sea

Smyrna

Hispalis

Carthago Nova

Mediterranean

Sicily

Athens

Hippo Regius

Carthage

VANDALS

Sea

Crete

BERBERS

to defend its borders or began bribing its barbarous neighbours to refrain from raiding. Some of this treasure found its way into Scandinavia by various means, and the social elite of the region was rich by anyone's standards during the period 400–600 AD.

Up until this time, the Scandinavians spoke the same language as other Germanic people, but changes between 550 and 750 AD resulted in the emergence of a language known as *dönsk tunga*, or 'the Danish Tongue', now called Old Norse. The Danish Tongue was spoken all across the 'Viking' lands of Denmark, Norway, Sweden, Britain, Iceland and the islands in between.

Later in the Viking era, a further divergence occurred between the language as spoken in eastern areas such as Sweden and Denmark, and regions farther west such as Iceland. At the time of that first raid on Lindisfarne, most Norsemen spoke the same tongue. This will have contributed to confusion about the exact origins of a particular raiding party.

ABOVE: The Vendel period gets its name from large archaeological finds dating from this era at Vendel in Sweden. This helmet came from a boat burial. Its construction indicates a high standard of metalworking skill.

The Vendel Period

The years between 400 and 800 AD were chaotic in much of Europe. The arrival of the Huns on the eastern fringes of Europe caused entire peoples to be displaced, pushing them westwards into their neighbours and bringing about an era of conflict as whole societies tried to find a new place to live.

This is known as the Migration Period, or *Völkerwanderung*, and the turmoil it caused lasted for centuries. By the eighth century AD a new order was emerging in Europe, with the powerful Merovingian kingdom controlling much of what had been Gaul. Scandinavia was not as badly affected by the Hunnic incursion as much of Europe, and continued to be relatively stable. Stability permitted trade and thus prosperity.

Sweden in particular was extremely wealthy at this time. A number of ship-burials discovered at Vendel (north of

OPPOSITE: Europe was turbulent in the period after the fall of the Roman Empire, with whole peoples displaced and forced into conflict with others as they sought a place to settle. Scandinavia was much less severely affected, permitting an era of relative prosperity.

ABOVE: **Cubbie Roo's castle on Wyre in the Orkneys was built after the end of the Viking Era by Norsemen who had lived in the Orkneys for centuries. Previously, Mesolithic and Neolithic people lived there, but had probably abandoned the islands long before the Vikings arrived around 600–700 AD.**

Stockholm) gave the era its modern name. These burials were magnificent in their extravagance, containing beautifully wrought items of gold, weapons and armour of high quality, and luxury goods that must have been imported into Scandinavia.

Burials and grave-goods of the Vendel period suggest that Scandinavia enjoyed an era of wealth and stability – but probably not peace, if the sagas of the time are to be believed – from 500 to 800 AD. Its people were able to afford trading expeditions into Europe and exploration into the eastern lands that are today Finland and Russia, as well as forays across the North Sea. Settlements were constructed in the Orkney Islands as a stopover on the 'sea roads' used for trading expeditions.

Dawn of the Viking Age

In 789 AD, not many years before the Lindisfarne raid, three 'Viking' (probably Norwegian) ships put into Weymouth on what is widely accepted as having been a trading expedition. A dispute with a local official became a brawl, and the brawl became a deadly fight with swords and axes. Although sometimes portrayed as a Viking raid on the port, this was probably more of an unintended international incident. Conflict with foreign sailors was at the time not uncommon. Piracy and raids against coastal

settlements occurred on a fairly frequent basis, and it was not
unknown for pirates to venture up rivers and attack towns further
inland. The 'merchants' involved in the incident at Weymouth
may well have been on a trading expedition at that time, but
that does not mean that they did not raid on other occasions.

This theme was repeated throughout
the Viking Age. Tough, well-armed
men in seaworthy ships were capable of
peaceful exploration and trade, or brutal
pillage and rapine. Which activity they
engaged in at any given time was perhaps a matter of personal
preference in some cases, but more often it was simply a question
of which was more profitable.

'FEAR NOT DEATH, FOR THE HOUR OF YOUR DOOM IS SET AND NONE MAY ESCAPE IT'.

There is some debate as to the origins of the word 'Viking'.
There is strong evidence that it derived from a word meaning
'expedition': a sea voyage requiring that the ship's rowers worked
in shifts. This was necessary on any longer journey, so any long-
distance exploration, trade or raiding would require such an
arrangement and would therefore be a 'Viking' expedition.

Whatever the origins of the word, it has come to be applied
to those who set out on voyages from Scandinavia in a particular
type of ship. The term became a word for sea-raiders and
ferocious warriors who worshipped barbarous gods. It has been
ever more loosely applied to the inhabitants of Scandinavia
during the Viking Age, including peaceful farmers who never
went near the sea. Outsiders knew only of what they had seen
in their contact with the Vikings, which was often violent.

Plunder and Profit

The Vikings, then, were a hardy and warlike people who had
developed a high standard of technology. They were expert
weapon-makers and workers of metal, and could build excellent
ships. They would trade when it was more profitable than raiding,
and they did not destroy for the sake of it – there was no profit in
that. The Vikings were driven by the same motivations that had
always inspired their people: wealth and word-fame. A successful
expedition – whether trading or raiding – would bring its
participants both of these precious commodities. A triumphant

OPPOSITE: **Early Viking raids were characterized by being small in scale and limited in penetration. It was relatively easy to follow the coast until a suitable target was located.**

return with a ship full of booty and tall tales of prowess in battle might be more exciting than a well-negotiated trade with far-off people, but the admiration of those looking upon the proceeds was not necessarily greater. A profitable voyage would inspire fame, which brought a status that could not always simply be bought with wealth.

The decision to launch the Lindisfarne raid was therefore logical. The target was an easy one, with prospects of a large quantity of plunder. The expedition offered everyone involved the chance to enrich himself both materially and in reputation.

'BETTER TO FIGHT AND FALL THAN TO LIVE WITHOUT HOPE'.

It appealed to an adventurous people who believed that a man could take what he wanted, providing he had won it by strength and prowess. From the point of view of the Scandinavian seafarers of the time, Lindisfarne was nothing more or less than a perfect opportunity to do what they had been doing for centuries.

The beginning of the Viking Age was not marked by a sudden departure from previous habits. The Vikings had been raiding and trading for generations. The only thing that really changed was the scale of their operations, and the amount of attention they attracted from those in a position to record history. The beginning of the Viking Age was not the moment when the Norsemen decided to start raiding; it was the moment that the rest of the world had to start taking notice.

BELOW: **The Viking longship was an efficient and seaworthy design, but it was a small craft in which to undertake long voyages on the open sea. Such vessels made more or less routine crossings to Iceland.**

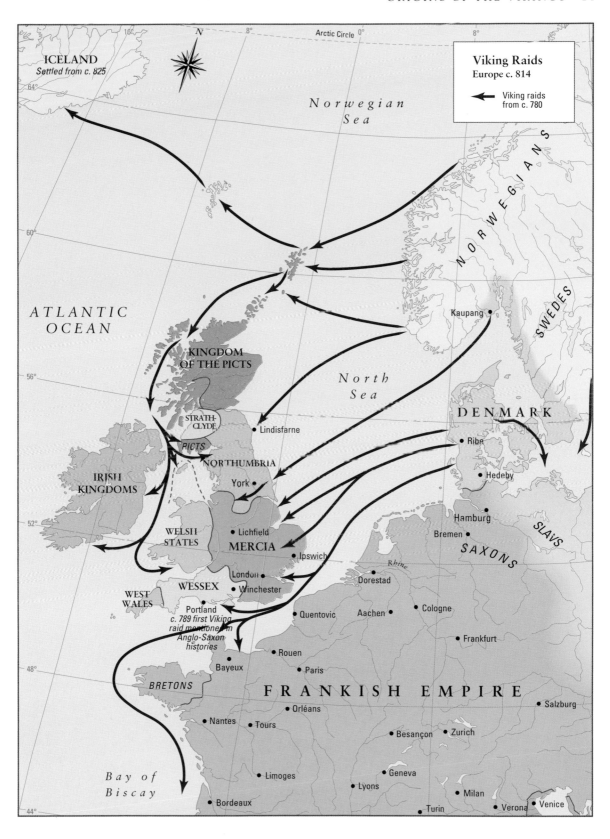

Arctic Circle

ICELAND
Settled from c. 825

64°

*Norwegian
Sea*

60°

N O R W E G I A N S

SWEDES

Viking Raids
Europe c. 814

Viking raids
from c. 780

**ATLANTIC
OCEAN**

Kaupang

56°

**KINGDOM
OF THE PICTS**

*North
Sea*

DENMARK

STRATH-
CLYDE

Lindisfarne

Ribe

PICTS

NORTHUMBRIA

Hedeby

**IRISH
KINGDOMS**

York

Hamburg

52°

Bremen

SLAVS

WELSH
STATES

Lichfield

MERCIA

SAXONS

Ipswich

London

Rhine

Dorestad

WEST
WALES

WESSEX

Winchester

Portland
*c. 789 first Viking
raid mentioned in
Anglo-Saxon
histories*

Quentovic

Aachen

Cologne

Frankfurt

Rouen

48°

Bayeux

Paris

BRETONS

F R A N K I S H   E M P I R E

Salzburg

Orléans

Nantes

Tours

Besançon

Zurich

Limoges

Geneva

*Bay of
Biscay*

Lyons

Milan

Verona

Venice

44°

Bordeaux

Turin

2

THE OLD NORSE RELIGION

The Vikings are often depicted as worshipping bloodthirsty gods, whose dark pagan rites involved human sacrifice and other abominable practices. This view was largely that of the Christian Church, but there is, however, some truth in it. Sacrifices were made, and there was a dark element to the Vikings' beliefs.

The Old Norse religion considered that the cosmos was in three major segments, which were subdivided into other lands. The world inhabited by mortal men was known as Midgard, the 'middle world', and was surrounded by a vast ocean. Beyond this ocean, which was huge but not necessarily impossible to cross, lay Utgard, the 'outer world' within which was Jotunheim, the land of the giants. To the north of Midgard were Nidavellir, home of the dwarves, and Svartálfheim, home of the dark elves. Under the ocean lived Jörmungandr, the 'world serpent'.

Below this 'middle world' centred on Midgard was Niflheim, land of the dead, and possibly Muspelheim, land of the fire

OPPOSITE: Odin's eight-legged steed Sleipnir was the very best of all horses, able to carry his master to Hel and back. He resulted from one of the adventures of the trickster god Loki, who became his mother whilst transformed into a mare.

giants. The location of Muspelheim is vague in Norse mythology; it may have lain to the south of Midgard, close to Niflheim, or somewhere else entirely. Above Midgard and connected to it by the Rainbow Bridge, Bifrost, were the lands of the gods, Vanaheim and Asgard, and also a land named Alfheim where the light elves lived.

The worlds of Norse mythology were connected by the world tree, Yggdrasil, which had roots in Jotunheim, Asgard and Niflheim. Yggdrasil was an ash tree apparently older than the universe, and which would survive even Ragnarök (the Twilight of the Gods, a great calamity involving the deaths of many gods and the submersion of the world before its rebirth). The only two people to survive the destruction of everything would be sheltered by the world tree.

Norse religion revolved around eternal conflict. There were two groups of gods, the Vanir and the Aesir, who were at war with the giants, and their final battle would destroy the universe. The Norse word for these enemies was *Jotnar*, which may have been similar to 'Titan' in Greek mythology but which has translated into English as 'giant.' The Aesir were descended from the giants and various gods married the children of giants, which implies kinship of some sort.

BELOW: The great ash tree Yggdrasil is central to Norse cosmology, with roots in different worlds. Yggdrasil survives even Ragnarök, sheltering the last humans from the destruction of the whole universe.

BAXTERS Patent Oil Printing 11 Northampton Square

Gods in Conflict

As if battling giants were not enough to keep the gods busy, there were also conflicts between the Vanir and the Aesir, the two races of deities. The Aesir were warriors and the Vanir were fertility gods. At first they lived in harmony in a golden age, playing games with golden pieces in pleasant meadows. Conflict eventually broke out between the Aesir and the Vanir.

The battle began with Odin, leader of the Aesir, hurling a spear into the ranks of the Vanir. This first spear-cast became a tradition in Viking warfare, with a good cast being seen as an omen of victory. In this case, however, it was not. The Vanir were able to destroy the walls of Asgard, home of the Aesir, with magic. The Aesir retaliated by toppling the walls of Vanaheim, where the Vanir lived.

'IT OFTEN HAPPENS THAT HE WHO GETS A DEATH WOUND YET AVENGES HIMSELF.

Eventually, it became obvious that neither side could win a decisive victory, so it was agreed that while there was wrong on both sides, much honour and respect were due to both the Vanir and the Aesir for their prowess and courage displayed in battle. Both sides agreed to negotiate a peace, with the Aesir coming off best in a deal that was nevertheless accepted by both sides. The result was an alliance of war and fertility gods who complemented one another well.

Once the war between the Aesir and the Vanir was concluded they lived in relative harmony, but personal conflicts among the gods were not uncommon. These were often due to rivalries or enmities arising out of their origins. In fact, it is not unreasonable to view much of Norse mythology as the tribulations of a large and argumentative family whose distant branches are often, but not always, feuding with one another.

Elves, Dwarves and Norns

Other than humans, the races of the universe were also powerful beings to one degree or another. The light elves in particular were associated with the Aesir and lived close to them, while the dark elves dwelled in an underground realm. The elves were powerful beings, but less so than they had been in earlier eras. Humans did at times sacrifice to the elves, who could be generous friends or terrible enemies, but were far more reliant upon the gods for help and guidance.

Humans did not worship the dwarves, but recognized them as beings of power. They lived underground, away from sunlight that would turn them to stone, and guarded great secrets. Likewise, humans did not worship the giants but recognized their immense power. Other beings, such as various undead and supernatural spirits, haunted the mortal world. Some were worshipped and could bestow benefits on those who sacrificed to them. They could also be angered sufficiently to do harm.

'GOOD TO LOVE GOOD THINGS WHEN ALL GOES ACCORDING TO THY HEART'S DESIRE.'

According to Norse mythology, every individual had a fate determined by the Norns, three women who could see the future, the present and the past. Some legends speak of other Norns who would visit newborn babies and confer their fate. Some of these Norns were malicious and would doom the baby to a difficult life, while others brought good fortune.

The Valkyrja, or Valkyries, were also supernatural beings. They were 'choosers of the slain' who carried dead warriors from the battlefield. In recent times they have been depicted as beautiful shield-maidens who sometimes ride winged horses, and in some sagas they may be daughters of kings. However, the Valkyries' mounts are depicted as wolves in earlier accounts, and the Valkyries themselves are described as raven-like. Thus they may have originally been rather less attractive than the romanticized modern version.

The Valkyries

Valkyries sometimes assist mortal warriors in the Viking sagas, and some stories include accounts of Valkyries becoming lovers of mortal heroes and even having children with them. Some Valkyries appear to have been both mortal and supernatural, a seeming contradiction that is actually well in keeping with the rest of Viking mythology – the gods and other supernatural beings are part of the world and visit the mortal realms quite often. If gods and men interact on a frequent basis, perhaps the boundary between mundane and supernatural can become blurred.

When not actively participating in battle, the Valkyries carried fallen warriors away. Half were taken to Valhol (more

LEFT: The modern depiction of the Valkyries as warrior maidens may be based on the accounts in some sagas of them taking human lovers and being the daughters of kings. They may originally have been hags or resembled carrion beasts, which would make them less attractive to heroes seeking a companion.

commonly translated into English as Valhalla) and the others to Fólkvangr. These two places served similar purposes but were ruled over by Odin and Freyja respectively. There, the dead warriors would prepare for the great battle of Ragnarök by engaging in combat with one another. When not fighting they would feast and be served mead by Valkyries. Here, too, is a blurring of the distinction between men and gods – mortals who fell in battle would stand alongside the gods against supernatural foes at the end of days.

Women did not go to Valhalla or Fólkvangr, and their fate after death is less clear. It is possible that they would find a place on the holy mountain of Helgafjell. There, those who had not died in battle but did not go to Hel would live out an eternal

version of their mortal lives. Helgafjell was not a bad place, and was not violent; some accounts describe it as essentially a comfortable eternal retirement.

Those who went to Hel were not so lucky. The goddess Hel ruled over a harsh realm of punishment and torment from which there was no escape. Warriors who failed to die in battle were doomed to Hel, making a death from sickness or other natural causes something to be feared. This in part explains the famous Viking ferocity – death in battle was less to be feared than survival in some cases, and certainly being killed in a fight was not the worst thing that could happen.

ABOVE: Odin, like all Norse gods, is a rather complex personality. All-father and great leader, his is a definitively male role, yet he uses magic that is considered effeminate by his peers.

OPPOSITE: Ymer, depicted here as Thor encountered him, was the first of the ice giants and was eventually slain by Odin and his sons. The gods dismembered Ymer and used his body to make the world. His blood became the seas and his flesh the land.

The Viking Gods

The Vikings had many gods, of whom the chief was Odin, the 'All-Father', who is credited with creating humans and fathering many of the Aesir. He was a warrior but also had other functions in Norse mythology, such as guiding souls to the afterlife. Odin was a god of wisdom who made great sacrifices for knowledge. One of the things he learned was the manner of his own death, and, with the help of his two ravens Hugin and Munin, he heard of everything that happened in the world.

Odin came to know that the world would end in a great battle known as Ragnarök, during which the wolf Fenrir would swallow him. His son Vidar would then avenge him. Odin knew the fate of all the gods – who among them would survive Ragnarök and who would not – and also that the universe would be largely destroyed. His foreknowledge in some ways echoes the Norse warrior's fatalism: death is inevitable, but word-fame lasts forever.

Odin had two wives: Frigg and Jord. Frigg, one of the Aesir, was the goddess of motherhood and the mother's role in domestic life. She was the mother of several gods and goddesses and (in some tales) a sister to Thor. Jord, mother of Thor, was the Earth goddess and is otherwise known as Fjörgyn or sometimes as Earth.

Perhaps the most famous of the Norse gods was Thor, the thunder-god who personified the Viking warrior in many ways. Thor spent much of his career battling giants, and in the legend of Ragnarök it was said that he and the world-serpent Jörmungandr would slay one another. He was a proud and rather angry god who was not known for his vast intellect. On one occasion he engaged in a traditional insult-contest with an individual who turned out to be a disguised Odin. While losing a battle of wits to the god of wisdom is not particularly damning, Thor failed to realize that he had been defeated.

Heimdall was another warrior god, although there are conflicting accounts of his deeds and role. His father was Odin and he had no less than nine mothers, all of them giants. Some tales suggest that Heimdall was the father of mortals, and he was known for his keen senses. He could stand on Bifrost, the rainbow bridge that connects Midgard to Asgard, and listen to the grass growing in Midgard. His role was to act as guardian of the bridge. On the day of Ragnarök he would give warning of the giants' approach and summon the gods to fight their last battle.

Not all the Norse gods were warriors, of course. Freyr and his sister Freyja were fertility gods who blessed mortals with prosperity and were celebrated as the bringers of peace. They were of the Vanir, given to live among the Aesir as hostages after the war between the two groups of gods ended. They brought with them magical treasures that proved useful to the gods.

Njord, father of Freyr and Freyja, was another Vanir hostage who lived among the Aesir in Asgard. He was a sea-god who could grant his worshippers safe voyages and prosperity gained from their

BELOW: A depiction of Heimdall, guardian of Bifrost, sounding his Gjallarhorn to warn the gods of the approach of their enemies. Thus begins Ragnarök, the apocalyptic battle between the gods and the Jotun that will end with the destruction of the universe.

journeys. He was not the only god of the sea; as seafarers, the Vikings naturally worshipped several sea-related gods, including Aegir, a friendly and hospitable god who brewed vast quantities of ale for the other gods. His wife Ran was not so pleasant; her task was to gather dead seafarers from the seabed in her nets and take them to the afterlife. Ran and Aesir had nine daughters who were represented as waves.

ABOVE: **Aegir, god of the sea, watches a Viking ship while his wife Ran lurks beneath the surface to gather up any who die by drowning. Their daughters are depicted as waves.**

Loki the Prankster

A large proportion of the troubles suffered by the Viking gods were the doing of Loki, child of giants but foster-brother (or perhaps blood-brother) to Odin. Loki was always a liar and was famed for playing pranks, some of them quite cruel, on the other gods and goddesses. However, at first he was also useful in their

ABOVE: **A soapstone carving of the face of Loki. Although the architect of Ragnarök and the deaths of most of the gods, Loki is a complex character who is also essential to the gods' survival on some occasions.**

struggles and helped his kin overcome many dangers, despite causing troubles by breaking their trust and engineering disputes. Loki's changing personality in many ways reflects his nature; the other gods were reliable and unchanging, but Loki evolved from a troublesome kinsman to a deadly foe.

Among Loki's misdeeds was the theft of the golden apples that kept the gods young. The Norse gods were not immortal, and staved off aging by eating magical apples. Tricked and hurt by the giant Pjazi, who was disguised as an eagle at the time, Loki agreed to steal the apples and the goddess Iounn who tended them. Deprived of their power, the gods aged and became weakened. They realized that Loki was responsible for their troubles and forced him to attempt a rescue. Loki took the form of a hawk and retrieved Iounn and her apples, returning to Asgard pursued by the giant who was then killed by the vengeful gods.

Loki was also responsible for the death of the god Baldr, although he did take advantage of a rather unwise hobby that various gods had taken up. Baldr was disturbed by dreams of his death, and his mother Frigg tried to protect him by making everything on Earth promise never to harm her young son. Everything thus swore, except mistletoe. Baldr's invulnerability became legendary, and the gods came up with a game in which they would hurl weapons at him. Loki made a spear or arrow out of mistletoe and gave it to Baldr's brother Hoor during their game, causing Baldr to be killed.

After a huge funeral Baldr went to the underworld, and his mother Frigg pleaded with Hel for his release. Hel agreed, on the

'WHO CAN'T DEFEND THE WEALTH THEY HAVE MUST DIE, OR SHARE WITH THE ROVER BOLD'.

condition that everything in creation, living and dead, would weep for him. So highly regarded was Baldr that everything did so, all except Loki, who was disguised as a giantess. Since the giantess would not weep, Hel kept Baldr.

Loki eventually became hostile and vindictive, probably out of anger at the punishment he received for the worst of his pranks: his second-hand murder of Baldr and subsequent prevention of Baldr's resurrection by deceiving the other gods. For this he was chained in a cave with the venom of a snake dripping onto his face. Although his wife Sigyn protected him by catching the venom in a bowl, she had to empty it sometimes and when she did the poison burned Loki, who remained imprisoned until Ragnarök.

Loki was the traditional foe of Heimdall, who would warn the gods when Loki led the giants against them on the day of Ragnarök. The two had fought before but Ragnarök would be their last encounter, in which they slew one another. This is a common theme in Viking mythology – heroes and gods who die fighting or just after vanquishing their greatest foe. It may seem tragic from a modern perspective but to the Vikings a heroic death battling one's sworn enemy was the very best way to go – what remained to a warrior after his arch-nemesis was defeated? Any further deeds would be anticlimactic and he might even suffer the terrible fate of dying of old age, forgotten or eclipsed by younger warriors.

Thus Loki provided several of the Norse gods with a suitable ending to their tale. Heimdall died fighting a kinsman-

BELOW: Loki's loyal wife Sigyn tries to protect him from dripping venom during his punishment for Baldr's slaying. Every time she has to empty the bowl, venom drips on Loki's face and causes him to writhe in pain, causing earthquakes.

god turned to evil, and other gods were provided with their ultimate challenge by Loki's deeds. In this, he is one of the most important of the Norse gods – heroes are, after all, defined by the magnitude of the challenges they face. Loki was the father of three great monsters: Hel, who ruled over the dead, Jörmungandr, the world-serpent, and the wolf Fenrir, who would slay Odin at Ragnarök. It was Loki who led the giants against Asgard in the days of Ragnarök.

Most famous of Loki's monster-children was the wolf Fenrir, who became a serious threat. After two attempts to bind him failed, the gods resorted to trickery and dwarven magic. They bet Fenrir that he could not break a special rope that the dwarves

RIGHT: The god Tyr sacrificed his hand to convince Fenrir that he would be released once the gods won their bet that he could be bound. Triumph at the price of great sacrifice is a common theme in Norse mythology.

had made out of six magical ingredients, and as a token of good faith the brave god Tyr placed his hand in the wolf's mouth. If Fenrir could not break the rope, the gods promised that they would release him, with Tyr's hand as hostage. Unable to escape and refused release, Fenrir bit off Tyr's hand. The wolf remained bound but set up such a howling that the gods silenced him by jamming his mouth open with a sword. Fenrir remained bound until just before Ragnarök, when he escaped to kill Odin.

Magic

The Norse gods used a variety of magical transportation. Odin had a magical boat called *Skidbladnir*, which could carry all the gods yet fold up and fit in a pocket. Thor had a chariot pulled by goats, and Freyja had one pulled by cats. She also rode a giant boar at times. Odin rode the eight-legged horse Sleipnir, which was an unintended child of Loki. Sleipnir's birth resulted from one of several occasions that Loki helped the gods deal with a difficult problem.

After the war between the Vanir and the Aesir, the walls of Asgard were in ruins and the home of the gods lay open to attack by giants. A master builder offered to construct impregnable fortifications. The result was a bet that if the fortifications could be built by the first day of summer, the goddess Freyja would become the builder's wife and he would also be given the sun and the moon. This was a hefty payment, but the task was a large one.

The builder had help from the stallion Svadilfari, as his deal with the gods did not allow any other assistance. Nevertheless, the work progressed on schedule and the gods became suspicious that their builder was in fact a giant. This put them in a difficult position as the deal was binding, but the gods were not willing to honour it. The answer was to send Loki to work his trickery.

Transformed into a mare, Loki tempted Svadilfari away from his work. The stallion chased the mare and the giant builder

ABOVE: Only the most powerful of deities, such as Freyja, would use a chariot pulled by cats. It is possible that her ability to get cats to go in the same direction upon command is a subtle reminder of a Viking woman's dominance over the household.

chased the stallion trying to get him back to work, until the deadline for the fortifications was past. The giant's pay was forfeit under the terms of the deal, so Thor killed him. Loki returned some time later, having given birth to a foal. The young horse was named Sleipnir and gifted to Odin.

Some gods also used magical weapons. Odin was armed with the spear Gungnir, while Thor fought with a magical hammer named Mjölnir, which had a short handle, could be concealed under a cloak and would return to Thor's hand when thrown. Thor also had a belt named Meginjörd, which doubled his strength, and a set of iron gloves named Jarngreipr that allowed him to wield Mjölnir.

The dwarves made many of the magical treasures owned by the gods. This began when Loki decided, for reasons that presumably made sense to the god of trickery, to cut off the goddess Sif's hair while she slept. Sif's husband, Thor, made dire threats against Loki, who wisely offered to make amends. He visited the dwarves and asked them to make replacement hair out of gold, which they did. They also made the spear Gungnir and the ship *Skidbladnir* as additional gifts.

This triggered intense rivalry among the other dwarven smiths, who bet Loki that they could make the best gifts for the gods. The loser would lose his head, so there was a strong incentive to win the bet. Loki, naturally, interfered but was not able to prevent the golden boar Gullin-Borsti and the magical arm ring Draupnir from being perfect. He was able to distract one of the smiths enough that the hammer Mjölnir was not quite as intended.

BELOW: Thor was one of the more straightforward Norse gods; a bold and skilled warrior of no great intellect. He is associated with storms and thunder and with using strength and bravery to overcome any obstacle.

Although its magic was as mighty as the smith had hoped, the hammer's handle was strangely short. Nevertheless, the bet was won. Loki managed to wriggle out of the deal with his head still attached, although his mouth was sewn up.

Ragnarök

The end of the world, or Ragnarök, is known as the Twilight of the Gods or the Doom of the Gods. 'Doom' does not necessarily mean a bad fate, but it certainly does mean fate – preordained and inescapable. The end begins with *Fimbulvetr*, or *Fimbulwinter*; a period of constant winter and conflict. Wolves destroy the sun and the moon, all bonds are broken (including those binding Loki and Fenrir) and the dead return from Hel. Led by Loki, they set sail to attack the gods. Meanwhile, the ice and fire giants march, and both Fenrir and Jörmungandr join the onslaught.

Heimdall blows his horn to warn of the attack, and the gods muster to meet it. Alongside them stand the warriors of Valhol and Fólkvangr, the best fighting men of all history. The clash that ensues sees many of the gods slain or mortally wounded along with their traditional foes.

There are few survivors of Ragnarök. Gods, men and monsters are slain, with only two humans surviving to seek refuge in the world tree, Yggdrasil. The whole world is burned by the fire of the fire giant Surtr, and the land then sinks beneath the sea. All the lands of men and gods, and even the land of the giants, are destroyed.

'THAT WHICH HAS A BAD BEGINNING, IS LIKELY TO HAVE A BAD ENDING.'

Ragnarök is a fitting end to the lives of Norse gods. Not for them a comfortable retirement after slaying their ancient foes, or eternal life. Their ending is a blaze of glory that is echoed in the desire of Viking warriors to die in battle. Life is fleeting in Viking belief, but word-fame is eternal. Thor drowns in the venom of Jörmungandr after slaying the great serpent, but he has saved the world from it and in any case, what is there for a warrior god to do after such a deed? Thor's epic career is completed by a suitably heroic death.

ABOVE: **Gods and warriors battle the serpent Jörmungandr and the wolf Fenrir in the devastated world of Ragnarök. The price of victory is immense – virtually everyone and everything in the universe perishes.**

It is a similar story with many of the other gods. Odin goes knowingly to his preordained fate, which he has foreseen many times. He is swallowed by Fenrir, but immediately avenged when his son Vidar tears the wolf apart. Tyr and the hound Garm slay one another. Heimdall, who has watched so long for Loki's attack, battles his enemy to mutual extinction. He avenges the wreckage of the universe by slaying the architect of its destruction.

After the destruction of Ragnarök the world is born anew. The land rises back out of the sea, better and more fertile than before. Crops grow freely and the daughter of the Sun, no less bright and just as warm, takes her place in the sky over this new and wonderful world. The warriors of Valhalla and Fólkvangr return to life, and Baldr comes back from the dead to rule them. The sons of Odin and Thor inherit their fathers' weapons and enjoy a return to a golden age, as it was before the troubles of the gods ever began.

Thus Ragnarök is not an ending at all, but a rebirth of the world as it should have been. Those who fall are remembered in eternal word-fame for having purchased the new universe with their courage and suffering. Those who survive enjoy the golden age. The time spent in Valhalla or Fólkvangr is not, then, the warriors' final destination, but a period of waiting and preparation. Those who qualify to be taken by the Valkyries are rewarded by a chance to fight alongside their gods and win a place in a reborn universe.

The Twilight of the Gods is in many ways a metaphor for the personal Ragnarök that each Viking warrior faces when his time comes. His fate was decided long ago, just like those of his gods, and he goes to meet it with a brave heart, although he is spared the burden of foreknowledge that Odin carried. If it is his time, then he will die and go to wait for the day of Ragnarök. If not, then he can hope that there will be other battles.

It is not hard to see how these beliefs tended to produce fearless warriors who would face any odds and were not deterred by hardship. A hopeless battle was not something to be avoided; it was an opportunity to win undying word-fame in the mortal world and ultimately a place in the golden age after Ragnarök.

Funeral Rites

The Vikings believed that proper funeral rites were essential if the deceased soul were to move on to the afterlife. A suitable funeral ensured that the spirit did not remain to haunt the living, and would have its rightful status in the next life. Grave-goods were important to ensuring this status; archaeological studies of burial sites have contributed greatly to what we know about the Vikings and their way of life.

The 'Viking Funeral', with the corpse burned aboard a ship set adrift after being loaded with goods, is a well-known concept. However, funeral practices varied, ranging from a simple burial to ceremonial cremation on land or aboard a ship.

BELOW: **Thor is the slayer of Jörmangandr, and thus the saviour of what remains of the world. The price is his life; Thor survives just long enough to realize that he has vanquished his greatest foe before succumbing to the serpent's venom.**

Cremation was the standard practice in Scandinavia until the Iron Age, at which point burial became more common. There is some speculation as to why this came about, and the most likely explanation is contact with the people of Eastern Europe and the social influences that went with it. Both practices were followed at the same time, with cremation being more common in Norway and burial prevailing elsewhere. However, it is not uncommon to find burial and cremation sites side by side and clearly in use at the same time, so perhaps the manner of disposal was a matter of preference.

The nature of an individual's funeral reflected their personal status and wealth as well as the general level of prosperity at the time. Some burials of important leaders prior to the Viking Age were extremely lavish, while others were quite poor. It may be that these leaders possessed a considerable amount of wealth, but during hard times it may have been considered wasteful to bury items that the living could use.

BELOW: Ships played an important part in Viking funerals, whether buried or set ablaze. Some were sent out to sea before being lit, but it was also common to burn a ship on land as a giant funeral pyre. Only a very important person merited the destruction of such an expensive item as part of their funeral.

LEFT: Pagan and Christian faiths coexisted in the Viking world for many years. This tenth century mould is used to cast both crosses and the hammer symbol of Thor, and many Vikings would have had no issues with owning both.

There are periods when the graves of people whose standing in life was quite different both contain the same paucity of grave-goods, suggesting that the needs of the living may have outweighed those of the departed. A good sword might at the time have been hard to replace, in which case it had to remain above ground in the service of those still living and in need of a weapon.

'MORE PEOPLE PREFER THE WORSE SIDE OF A STORY WHICH HAS TWO VERSIONS'.

However, during the Viking Age and for most of the period leading up to it, grave-goods were common. A poor individual might have next to nothing, but most men were buried with their weapons and the tools of their craft; women with jewellery and household tools. Important figures such as nobles and religious leaders were given a lavish burial, with grave-goods that might include horses and even slaves sacrificed so that they might continue to serve.

Monuments such as standing stones and large barrow-mounds mark many Viking burial sites, and were not merely tombs but also status symbols for the deceased and their descendants. A large burial mound housing a high-status ancestor conferred a certain prestige on his kin living nearby and served as a constant reminder of his wealth and power. Monuments and impressive tombs were thus a part of the word-fame a Viking hoped to achieve. They ensured that for as long as anyone lived close by or

even just passed on their way, the living would be reminded of the tomb's owner.

The Viking sagas contain stories that serve as a warning about the consequences of an improper funeral. If not properly sent on their way to the next life, the dead might return as revenants or *draugr*. These unquiet dead must be put down in a manner similar to the traditional ways of disposing of a vampire – decapitation or a stake through the heart.

'THE COUNSEL OF FOOLS IS THE MORE MISGUIDED THE MORE OF THEM THERE ARE'.

Ships and Pyres

Ships played an important part in some funeral rituals. It may be that the ship was a symbolic vehicle for the journey to the next life, or perhaps it was simply a piece of grave-goods. A ship was an expensive item and time consuming to make. Anyone who could afford to have a ship buried with him – a ship filled with goods, at that – was indeed rich. Although it is popularly understood that a Viking funeral involves setting the ship adrift and burning it, ships were often buried.

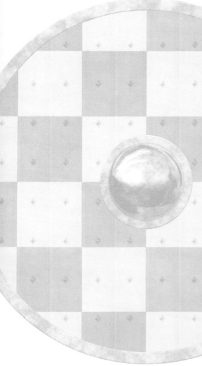

If the method of disposal was cremation, the fire had to be hot enough to destroy completely not only the corpse but also the grave-goods, presumably so that they would go with the owner and not be left behind in the mortal world. Ashes were then to be buried or scattered on the sea. In cases where the corpse was burned aboard a drifting ship, this function was carried out by nature; the burned remains of ship and man would be scattered by the wind to sink into the sea.

The funeral of the god Baldr, killed by the most vicious of Loki's pranks, echoes the traditional Norse funeral. A funeral pyre was built aboard Baldr's ship *Hringhorni* and his body placed atop it along with that of his wife, who had died of grief during the preparations. The god's favourite horse was sacrificed and also placed on the pyre so that Baldr would have additional transport in the afterlife. The pyre was lit and the ship set adrift.

Not only were Baldr's goods placed upon the pyre, but his father, Odin, also gave a rich gift. The arm-ring Draupnir, which created additional identical rings every few days and was one of

Odin's most prized possessions, was placed on Baldr's arm. This indicates the high esteem in which his father, Odin, and the other gods held Baldr. It may not have been common practice for others to give gifts for the deceased to take into the afterlife, although it may have happened with a well-loved relative or highly respected leader.

Odin is said to have whispered to Baldr before the pyre was lit, and in some legends Odin promises his son resurrection. This may have been a reference to the attempt by the gods to have Baldr released from Hel's domain, or perhaps Odin knew that his son would come back to life after Ragnarök and rule over mortals in the new golden age. Either way, Odin's promise of resurrection echoes the belief that those who die a good death and then play their part in Ragnarök will come back to life afterward and live in paradise. For this to be possible, however, preparation for burial or cremation had to follow certain rules, many of which were of mythical significance. The nails of the deceased were trimmed, since on the day of Ragnarök the dead would sail to war against the gods in a ship held together by the nails of dead men. Rites of this sort deprived the enemy of raw materials – even the preparation of the dead was part of the war between the gods and their foes.

Seven days after death a feast was held called *Sjaund*, which was also the name of the funeral ale that was drunk then. The heirs of the deceased met at the feast and settled his affairs, paying off creditors and resolving any outstanding issues that he had left behind. This was not always a particularly amicable business, and feuds could result; equally, they could also be

ABOVE: **An intact Viking ship excavated near Oseberg in Norway shows the advanced state of shipbuilding in the Viking era. An excellent balance of speed and carrying capacity, Viking ships were well suited to the coastal waters of Scandinavia where they originated.**

resolved at the *Sjaund*. Afterwards, the deceased was truly gone. His or her affairs were considered settled and the heirs received their inheritance.

Religious Practices: Sacrifices and Feasts

Viking religion before the coming of Christianity was a very personal affair rather than the formal structure that replaced it. Relatively little has been recorded about the Vikings' religious practices, and much of what is known is based on the undoubtedly biased reports of Christian observers. There are also dark legends of extremely unpleasant practices, although how much of this was in the interest of a good story and how much of it was actual day-to-day religion is open to question.

Sacrifices were made to the gods and spirits venerated by the Vikings, and these did at times include animal and human

RIGHT: A Viking leader goes to the afterlife with his ship and faithful horse as transportation. His armour, weapons and shield are ready for use, and he will likely have many precious objects to give him status in the next world. Funerals of this sort echo the rites given to the beloved god Baldr when he was slain by Loki's treachery.

offerings as part of the Viking religion. Sometimes the sacrifice was simple, such as the killing of a horse to place on its master's funeral pyre, and sometimes highly complex. The Islamic scholar Ibn Fadlan, who witnessed a Viking funeral, left a comprehensive account of the sacrifice of a young woman.

The sacrificial rites were sexual in nature, and involved a great deal of strong drink. During the ceremonies the girl bade farewell to her friends and family, and was treated with high honour. Ibn Fadlan records that she seemed happy during the feasting the night before her death. On the following day, she took part in a rite whereby she was lifted on what appeared to be a door frame to enable her to see into the mystical world, and there saw her family waiting for her along with her master at whose funeral she was to be sacrificed. She said that they beckoned her and were happy that she was coming to join her.

Just before being put to death, the girl had sex with several men in rapid succession and was then killed by strangulation and a knife thrust. Her death was apparently necessary to assist her master's passage into the next life, with her body acting as a vessel for life force. This kind of complex ritual sacrifice was not common, but may have reflected the high status of the leader at whose funeral it took place.

Even the gods were not exempt from sacrifice. Odin ritually impaled himself to a tree for several days to obtain his celebrated wisdom, and it was acceptable to sacrifice humans as well as animals. According to Adam of Bremen, writing in the eleventh century from second-hand sources, a great religious festival was held every nine years at Uppsala, Sweden, which included the sacrifice of nine men.

The number nine was highly significant to the Vikings, and so each day for nine days a human was sacrificed along with other species of animals. Sacrifices were hanged from trees in a sacred grove, in the manner of Odin's self-sacrifice. This took place at the beginning of summer, which was the traditional time for sacrifices to Odin. Normally, the human sacrifices were criminals and outlaws, or sometimes slaves. However, the sagas speak of a famine so desperate that the king was sacrificed to end it. This took place after the sacrifices of animals and then lesser men had failed to produce a result. These events are not dated, but they probably took place in the centuries before the dawn of the Viking Age.

'YOU WILL REACH YOUR DESTINATION EVEN THOUGH YOU TRAVEL SLOWLY'.

Other sacrifices were rather more mundane. Often they took the form of feasts that were celebrations and social as well as religious events. Feasts were held at the beginning, middle and end of winter. The first asked for divine aid in getting through the winter without famine. The second was intended to create auspicious circumstances for the new crops soon to be sown, and the third was dedicated to success in the year's ventures. These included any trade or raiding expeditions that might be launched. Feasts were also held on other occasions, not necessarily planned in advance. A feast might be held to ask for good fortune in a difficult time to come, or for an end to present troubles.

RIGHT: **The Vikings did not normally drink from horns, but it is possible that they were used on ceremonial occasions. A horn is a rather impractical device for day-to-day use.**

The feast was a fairly pragmatic business. Animals were sacrificed to the gods and then eaten, with both the killing and the consumption being part of the religious experience. The manner of sacrifice was usually to behead the beast with an axe, using a single powerful stroke. This required a fair amount of skill as well as strength, and was undoubtedly very messy. The spray of blood from the animal's severed neck was also part of the feasting ceremony, and blood was used to redden idols and the arm-ring used for oaths. Blood may also have been used to predict the future through the reading of omens, to create a symbolic link with the participants' dead ancestors, and possibly to ward off misfortune.

Copious amounts of ale was drunk in the honour of both gods and departed friends. Being mentioned at feasts long after death was part of the word-fame a warrior or explorer hoped to win. The head of the household, who served as both host and to some extent priest, blessed the ale.

Temples and Holy Sites

The Viking sagas contain descriptions of large and impressive temples, but there is little archaeological evidence of this. Most religious observances were probably made in the home or outdoors, at sites considered to be auspicious or holy. One such site was an island in the Black Sea, where it became traditional to give thanks to the gods for a safe voyage down the River Dnieper.

Many holy places were associated with trees, possibly in connection with Yggdrasil, the world tree. Others sites included waterfalls and particular stones or boulders. Not all of these sites were holy to the gods; some were associated with the land-spirits, or *Landvaettir*. These spirits protected those who venerated them and would provide natural bounty in the form of good hunting or plentiful crops. They could, however, be offended. Notably, an area where notorious bloodshed had occurred might be abandoned and avoided in case its land-spirits were angry or vengeful.

Idols were also used for worship. Some were statues of the gods while others were more abstract, such as carved markers. Ibn Fadlan wrote extensively of his interactions with Viking traders. He describes them giving offerings to a tall wooden idol carved with faces – possibly those of the gods – and asking for favours including contact with local traders who had too much money and would not haggle over prices.

Although the Vikings saw their gods as friends and relatives and were quite happy to curse or yell abuse at them for failing to provide favourable circumstances, it was not uncommon for individuals to prostrate themselves in front of idols or in holy places. From this position, the gods were beseeched to be kind

ABOVE: **An eighth century funerary stone depicting mythological scenes as well as parts of the sagas. The treatment of the deceased was an important matter for the Vikings; unquiet dead could come back to trouble the living, and would swell the ranks of the enemy at Ragnarök.**

or generous. This image of Viking religion fits well with their relationship with the gods – excessive respect to the point that grovelling was acceptable when asking for something, but so was outrage if it were not granted.

Various means were used to interact with the mystical world. Poems were used by seers to perform magic and to see into other worlds, and in *Egil's Saga*, one of the great Viking saga-poems, Egil composes a poem intended to inspire the land-spirits to assist him in taking vengeance against the king of Norway, Eric Bloodaxe. A curse might be used for the same purpose; later in the saga Egil tries again to get the spirits to assist him against Eric, this time by erecting a rune-carved pole as an insult to the spirits. He curses them to be unable to find rest or to return to their homes until they have helped him take his revenge.

Curses were also used to redirect misfortune and the disfavour of gods or supernatural beings. Some of the early settlers in Iceland were concerned not to offend the Landvaettir and used supernatural means to find a place to set up their home. The first settler into Iceland, Ingolf Arnarson, threw the pillars that supported his high-seat overboard from his ship, and attempted to follow them as they washed up on the shore. He was not able to do so, and set up a home while his servants searched for the pillars. Once they were found, Ingolf moved his home to their location. Although this was not the best land available, he felt that the gods had directed him to that spot and the local spirits would be welcoming rather than offended by his presence. It seems that he was right; modern Reykjavik, capital of Iceland, stands on the same site.

Lodmund the Old was not so fortunate. He, too, was unable to follow his high-seat pillars and, like Ingolf, set up a home. Some time later he was informed that his pillars had been found in a far-off part of Iceland. He immediately

BELOW: A statue of Ingolf Arnarson, leader of the first Viking settlers in Iceland. His decision to allow the gods to determine a favourable landing site seems to have been wise; over a thousand years later the capital of Iceland stands on the same spot.

re-embarked in his ship, and just in time. A landslide demolished Lodmund's home just after he left.

To prevent the misfortune from following him, Lodmund forbade anyone to speak his name and essentially hid from the Landvaettir so that they could not find him. He cursed the site of his old home, saying that no ship that sailed from there should ever find its destination. This presumably prevented the spirits' disfavour from following him; Lodmund's new house was built on the site where his pillars had washed up and was not visited by disaster.

The high-seat was a place of power in its own right. It was the place where the head of a Viking household sat, and had a pair of wooden pillars to either side of it. These pillars may have been carved with images of gods, although there is little information available to modern scholars about them. Religion and political power were intertwined, and the head of a household had spiritual authority as well as being a political leader.

ABOVE: **Arm-rings were a popular decorative item, displaying wealth and status. The dragon head seems also to have been a popular image and has become associated with the prows of Viking ships, although no surviving examples have been found.**

Holy sites, whether purpose-built temples or not, were considered sufficiently sacred that to enter one armed was sacrilege. A murder committed with a weapon in such a site was doubly serious as it was a breach of social custom and trust as well as being sacrilegious to the gods. Anyone who did violence in a holy place became an outlaw. This prohibition, obviously, did not apply to the holy places of other religions.

Temples and holy sites were important to trade and diplomacy as well as spiritual matters. Each holy place was required by law to have a silver arm-ring that was worn by the local chieftain, or *Godi*. The ring was used for the swearing of oaths for all manner of reasons, not least to formalize trade bargains. The Godi occupied a position somewhere between priests and nobles or chiefs, providing both religious and political leadership. They led the worship of the gods and appointed officials as well as making laws.

3

VIKING LAW AND SOCIAL ORDER

The Vikings are often portrayed as lawless savages who lived only to slaughter their enemies (or simply anyone they encountered) and to steal whatever they could. In reality, if this had been the case they would have been no threat to anyone outside their immediate vicinity.

It takes an organized society to launch any kind of expedition, let alone project an effective military force across a wide expanse of sea. While Viking society varied somewhat from place to place and time to time, it was always anything but lawless. Indeed, it was said about the Icelandic Vikings that they had no king other than the law. Viking laws formed the basis of Icelandic law, and probably influenced the development of laws throughout Scandinavia and all regions where the Norsemen settled.

Law of some kind is absolutely necessary to the long-term survival of a society. On a small scale, social custom and the orders of a powerful individual can suffice, but as the number

OPPOSITE: The site of the original Althing is today a national park. It was here that the people of Iceland gathered to formulate laws and settle disputes in a democratic and civilized manner.

of people involved grows, so it becomes necessary to have well-understood laws and a means of enforcing them. Without such a structure to support it, society will collapse into a tangle of self-interest and violence as the strong prey on the weak.

It is easy to think of the Vikings as a warrior culture in which the strong did indeed prey on the weak, but a warrior needs the support of a society to feed him and – more importantly – to support the industries that arm and equip him. A swordsmith cannot ply his trade if he is constantly fending off attacks on his property or attempting to obtain food to survive, and without skilled swordsmiths there would be no weapons for the warriors.

Law-Abiding Citizens

The process that put a sword in the hand of a Viking warrior was a complex one, governed and made possible by law. The swordsmith was able to buy food and clothing using the proceeds of his labour. The farmers who provided the food were able to sell their surplus for money, including that of the swordsmith, but that money had to have some value if the farmers were to want it.

Laws that punished merchants for cheating their clients helped ensure that trade remained desirable. If not, society would eventually collapse back to a personal subsistence level. Laws that protected the farmer, the merchant and the swordsmith ensured that they were able to go about their business reasonably unhindered, and thus kept the fabric of society intact.

There was no police force, of course: armed men enforced the law using the swords that the law had put in their hands. Law provided stability, and stability often translated to prosperity. A prosperous society could afford to be well armed and strong, and so long as that strength was used in a manner that did not disrupt the fabric of society, the system was self-perpetuating. The law helped ensure that this was the norm, as much as possible.

Prosperity also made possible the great expeditions of exploration and trade – and raids for plunder – that gave the Vikings their name and reputation. Most 'warriors' were not full-time soldiers, and spent most of their time as farmers or in other non-violent occupations. Only a small segment of any society can be employed in areas that do not directly contribute to the

economy, so most Vikings took up arms only when they needed
to or when there was an economic reason.

A good raid or a successful trading expedition could produce
more wealth than the same period tilling the land, and the
law made it possible to leave the farm for a time. It would be
protected by the rest of society, freeing up the householder for
his expedition. A stable society governed by law also ensured
that when he returned, the successful Viking would be able to
sell his plunder or proceeds for the things that he needed.

Most laws, in any society, exist for the defence of that
society against actions that would damage either society itself or
individuals within it. Enough attacks on individuals will disrupt
society anyway, so laws that protect people and their property are
good for the overall social order. Similarly, laws that provide for
the resolution of disputes, and which force the parties involved
to accept and abide by the decision, are also good for society, as
they, too, prevent social disruption.

Such laws are also good for the individuals that live
under them. The resolution of a dispute might go against an
individual, but at least he is less likely simply to be murdered
by the other party. An ongoing dispute could be damaging to
local society and economic activity, which would harm the
whole nearby community.

ABOVE: **Most Vikings
lived in small farming
communities similar
to this reconstructed
site. The head of the
household may have
been absent for long
periods on a raiding or
trading expedition, but
afterward he would
return to his farm and
resume his duties.**

OPPOSITE: **The sword
was a status symbol as
well as a weapon. Only
the most successful or
powerful men could
afford a sword, although
a warrior might be gifted
with one by his Jarl
or perhaps win one as
booty in a raid or feud.**

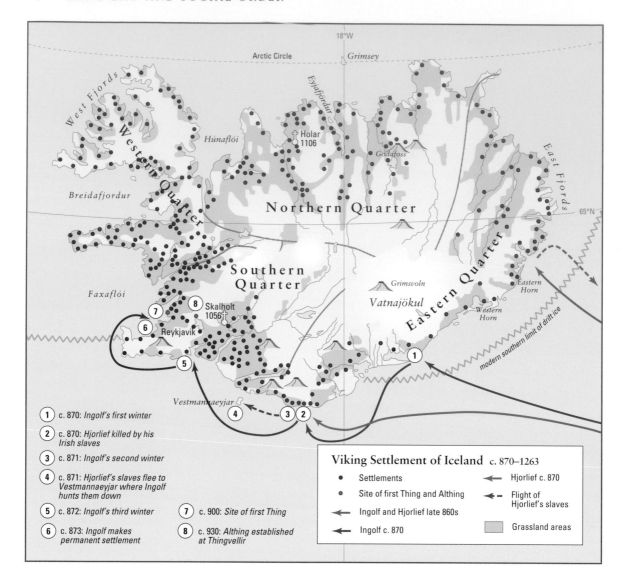

Arctic Circle   Grimsey
18°W

West Fjords

Western Quarter

Húnaflói   Holar
1106

Godafoss

East Fjords

Breidafjordur

Northern Quarter   65°N

Southern
Quarter

Grimsvoln   Eastern
Horn

Faxaflói   Vatnajökul   Eastern Quarter   Western
Horn

⑧ Skalholt
⑦   1056⚓   modern southern limit of drift ice

⑥ Reykjavik

⑤

①

Vestmannaeyjar

④   ③②

1 c. 870: Ingolf's first winter

2 c. 870: Hjorlief killed by his Irish slaves

3 c. 871: Ingolf's second winter

4 c. 871: Hjorlief's slaves flee to Vestmannaeyjar where Ingolf hunts them down

5 c. 872: Ingolf's third winter

6 c. 873: Ingolf makes permanent settlement

7 c. 900: Site of first Thing

8 c. 930: Althing established at Thingvellir

Viking Settlement of Iceland c. 870–1263	
• Settlements	← Hjorlief c. 870
• Site of first Thing and Althing	◄- - Flight of Hjorlief's slaves
← Ingolf and Hjorlief late 860s	▨ Grassland areas
← Ingolf c. 870	

ABOVE: **Settlers arriving in Iceland pushed inland from the coast, using waterways as passage. The pattern of settlement reflects not only the location of the best land, but also the routes taken to reach it.**

The Vikings benefited from a functional legal system in which individuals had considerable input. More is known about the situation in Iceland than elsewhere, but since Iceland was settled from Scandinavia it is not unlikely that a similar system existed there. Many laws were made at meetings named *Things*, which took place at intervals of (usually) one year.

The Althing

Things were held at the local and regional level, and in Iceland the *Althing* was a national event. The Thing was a major social occasion and a period of truce. The Althing site was considered a holy place, making it both socially unacceptable and also sacrilegious to carry weapons there. Laws were discussed and agreed at the Thing, along with disputes that were resolved if possible. These were democratic events, in which all free men who met certain conditions (basically being reasonably sound in body and mind) were permitted to speak their thoughts and to have a say in what was decided. In Iceland, where the settlers did not want a king or other ruler, the laws agreed at the Althing were the highest authority in the land.

The Althing was open to all free men, although it was mainly a meeting between the Godi (chieftains). In each

'THERE'S NO EXCUSING THE MAN WHO REJECTS THE TRUTH ONCE IT'S PROVEN'.

of the four main regions of Iceland there were nine Godi, who acted as representatives and protectors of those who gave their allegiance. Allegiance could be shifted from one Godi to another, and a chieftain had responsibilities towards his supporters just as they were required to fight in his support if necessary.

Normally, the Godi of a region held a Thing in the spring and then took wider issues to the Althing in the summer. Each Godi had two or more advisors, and might bring a significant body of armed men as protection or additional influence if he were involved in a serious dispute. At the Althing, an appointed Lawspeaker recited one-third of the laws in force. He held his post for three years, so in the course of his term he was required to learn all of his society's laws.

The replacement of the Lawspeaker, which was a paid position, ensured that no one became entrenched in the post and used his influence over a long period, and also made sure that the body of law was not housed in a single individual. If something happened to the current Lawspeaker, hopefully previous post-holders would be available. They could also remind local Godi of the law, even if they no longer spoke it at the Althing.

Although any free man could be heard at the Althing, it was the Godi and their advisors who finally agreed what laws to put into place and how to apply them. This gathering was also empowered to make agreements with foreign powers if such a need arose, although this was rare as Iceland was remote and received few visitors. Most interaction with foreigners was on a small-scale and fairly individual basis, and was conducted by shiploads of Vikings as they thought best.

Legal Disputes

Disputes were resolved at the Althing by a council of 36 judges appointed by the Godi. They were in many ways also a jury; for a case to be decided, 30 of the judges had to agree or at least not oppose the decision. This system was amended later to allow deadlocked cases to be referred to a new court, which would decide by simple majority.

Legal cases were brought in the manner of modern civil suits to some extent; there were no state-vs-individual prosecutions as such. Criminal acts were thus dealt with as if they were disputes between an individual and the person he believed had wronged him. However, anyone could bring a case before the court, even if he were not involved. Thus many injustices were dealt with even if the hurt party was unwilling or too frightened to raise the case.

Witnesses in a legal hearing were required to swear oaths not only about the truthfulness of what they said, but also agreeing to abide by the legal procedures that they were taking part in. Everyone involved was bound by oaths, and perjury was harshly punished. It was possible for a case to be won or lost on legal technicalities, notably the following of correct procedures in keeping with the oaths sworn to do so, which an unscrupulous opponent could easily exploit.

In one saga, the defendant is summoned to court to speak in his own defence but his way is blocked by his opponent's followers. His men force their way through and manage to arrive in time. Had they failed to do so, the court would have found against the defendant not because of any evidence of guilt, but due to his failure to follow correct procedure.

Outlawry

The courts could sentence the guilty party to be given as a slave to the individual he had wronged, or could declare the defendant an outlaw. This was a very serious matter, although it was not a punishment as such since the court itself would not immediately

act against the guilty party. However, outlawry placed the criminal outside the protection of the law. He could be killed by anyone who felt like it without penalty, and all members of society were forbidden to offer him shelter or support.

In some cases the period of outlawry was for three years, after which, if the guilty party survived, he could return to his place in society. His chances of survival were reasonable at most, but at least he had some safe places to rest. The outlaw was permitted three places of safety and could not be attacked so long as he remained within bowshot of one of them. He was also safe on the road between them, although he had to move off the road to allow others to pass and not come within spear-length of them.

An individual who was fully outlawed had no such safe havens. He was banished forever and his property was confiscated. This was more or less a death sentence, as life would be very hard for someone cast out of society. He was safe

ABOVE: The Althing was a major social event as well as a legal and governmental one. The annual meeting of people from all parts of Iceland resulted in the emergence of a common culture, with no region developing in isolation.

nowhere; there were plenty of men who sought the glory of killing outlaws to increase their own status. Outlawry was also, to some extent, a legally sanctioned invitation to the wronged or his friends and family to take vengeance on their enemy. Thus the outlaw might be actively hunted by his enemies, while also facing hardship from the environment and the occasional attack by outlaw-hunters.

Full outlawry was a harsh sentence reserved for the worst of offenders, such as kin-slayers. Killing a relative was considered to be a terrible crime, perhaps because of the traditional trust between family members. Even a period of three years was a long time to be without the protection of law, and many offenders did not survive for long.

Many legal disputes stopped short of outlawry and instead resulted in the award of a compensation payment from the guilty party. Law and custom set levels of compensation for various offences, so once the court had decided that someone was guilty the sentence was automatic. However, there was no formal provision for collection of the payment, which was not enforced by the court. The winner of the case had to take care of collection of payment.

Failure to pay compensation would of course be grounds for a new legal case, which might result in a different penalty or another refused payment. However, if the guilty party failed to make his payment, others might look badly upon him and the injured party would be seen as justified in acting against him. This could result in harassment or violence, perhaps leading to an ongoing feud.

'WARD THY WORDS WELL, FOR THEY MAY SEEM MORE HASTY LATER, THAN THEY DO NOW.'

The courts were not the only way to resolve a dispute, of course. Often a settlement was made with or without the arbitration of a third party, simply by discussing the matter and agreeing a resolution. Alternatively, one party might simply ask the other to dictate the terms of a resolution. There were various reasons why this might be done, and not just because one party was powerless. A request for a dictated solution could be almost a challenge of honour; a harsh resolution might reflect badly on a man who wanted to be seen as generous by his community, so he might be compelled to fairness by social pressure.

Bitter Feuds

Another way to resolve disputes was to fight. Violence was often part of a dispute, especially where a feud existed, but could also be used to force an end to the problem. A brawl or even an armed clash might not have any real consequences beyond injuries suffered, but could escalate into a lengthy feud. They could also result from a simple insult or the escalation of a dispute.

For example, the Icelandic sagas mention incidents where men went to their chieftains, who were rivals, with a grievance. This brought the chieftains into direct conflict, and what had up to that point been a small matter was escalated into a bloody clash between armed parties.

A feud was socially acceptable and was often seen as necessary to restore honour after an insult or to take vengeance for a crime. It essentially took the form of small war declared between the feuding parties. There were rules in place governing who was allowed to take part in a feud, which went some way towards preventing a minor incident from expanding to include every kinsman, friend and neighbour of the feuding parties, plus anyone else they could persuade to help out.

A feud could simmer for a long time, especially where the enemies were well matched and needed to be cautious about attacking one another. Without a clear advantage, escalating the level of violence was highly risky and while Viking men were not overly concerned with personal safety, losing a feud might have consequences beyond simply dying in battle.

Feuds were characterized by acts of violence, even when started by something as trivial as a perceived insult. Once the feud had started, the family, friends and supporters of the feuding parties were fair game and might be attacked or killed. Raids to steal cattle and incidentally do violence to the enemy were also possible. If a member of one feuding party was killed, vengeance against at least one member of the other side was necessary for the sake of honour.

A feud of this sort could go on for a long time, and although there were laws governing who was involved (it was utterly dishonourable, for example, to attack women), there was a real danger that the best fighting-men would be killed in a long-running feud. These individuals were usually also prosperous householders and economically important members of the community, so feuding could be damaging to society.

Duels and Vengeance

One way to prevent a feud developing was a duel. The original form of Viking duel was the *Einvigi*. This was a straight fight with no rules; the combatants fought with whatever weapons they had and there were no officials as such. In other societies, especially in Europe in later centuries, there were kinds of niceties associated with the duel – matched weapons, conventions as to what was and was not allowed, and so forth. The Vikings simply met up at a prearranged time and tried to kill one another.

It is notable that while a Viking expecting to fight a duel might ask the gods for strength or other assistance, the duel itself had no religious significance. This was no judicial duel or trial by combat; the victor won through his own strength, cunning and skill at arms. Victory proved nothing more than that he was better at fighting than his opponent and was not seen as proof of divine favour or lack of guilt. It did, however, honourably settle the matter and might, hopefully, end the feud.

BELOW: The Einvigi duel was a fair fight in that the rules were the same for everyone – a combatant could use whatever weapons and armour he possessed. This did mean that at times a better-equipped duellist had a significant advantage.

Vengeance against the victor of a duel was acceptable. Killing someone in the course of a feud would usually result in at least an attempt at vengeance, but if the death occurred in a properly declared duel, matters were slightly different. Not all duels resulted in death, of course, but in those cases where a combatant died, his kin were entitled to

LEFT: The Holmgang duel was more even-handed than the Einvigi, in that the weapons and equipment to be used were agreed before the combat began. In theory a Holmgang was more survivable than an Einvigi duel, but a skilled fighter could deliver a death-blow before the fight was stopped.

redress. This could take the form of *weregeld*, or blood-price, if the family of the dead combatant were prepared to accept it.

Weregeld was a payment made to the kin of the deceased as recompense, and acceptance ended the matter. It was thus a useful way to prevent feuds from developing out of a duel, just as the duel offered an alternative to going straight from harsh words to an attempt to massacre one another's families. Weregeld could be paid as recompense for offences other than killing someone, and was set by law at a level depending on the social status of the slain individual or the property damaged. There was no negotiation about the level of weregeld, just the decision whether or not to accept it.

Individuals might be keen on the idea of a duel as a ticket to Valhol and might even go around picking fights as they aged, hoping to avoid the awful fate of dying in bed. This was potentially damaging to society, however, and in an effort to reduce the number of fatalities a new kind of duel was introduced in Norway and Iceland. This was the *Holmgang*.

The Holmgang duel was much more formal than the Einvigi. The combatants fought in an area delineated by cloaks spread on the ground, and were forbidden to retreat or step off the cloaks. Each was armed with a sword that may have been of a special design associated with the duel. It was permissible to take a second sword into the duel, hanging on a thong from the wrist. Each combatant had a rather flimsy shield, and a shield-bearer stood by with two spares. He passed replacements over when one was destroyed.

The combatants took turns to strike at one another, with the challenged party striking first. Once a shield was reduced to splinters the next was used until the duellist ran out. Thereafter he defended with his sword and at this point a second weapon would be highly useful if the duellist thought to bring one. The Holmgang duel was, in theory at least, intended to be non-fatal and was stopped when blood flowed on the cloaks underfoot. Whoever was worst injured at that point was the loser.

'WHEN SOMEONE SPEAKS OF ILL, IT IS NEVER FAR AWAY. '

Normally a Holmgang duel took place at a customary spot, and many communities had a regular duelling ground. When the challenge was made and accepted, it was agreed what the loser would pay to the winner, and this payment sealed the matter. However, if the winner of a Holmgang duel slew his opponent, he received all his goods. Since only a serious wound stopped the fight, this was quite hard to achieve. The duellist would have to achieve a killing blow or a mortal wound in a single strike that his opponent knew was coming. A considerable degree of skill – or blind luck – would be necessary for such a blow.

Dueling Variations

Variations on the Holmgang did occur. There are accounts in the sagas where duellists used weapons other than swords, such as spears and axes. These stories are not necessarily true, however. Later writers sometimes confused the Holmgang and the Einvigi, so a reference to a duel with axes or spears might not be a formal Holmgang. Even when the conventional sword and shield were used a certain degree of skulduggery was possible. It was not permissible for the shield-bearer to attack, but he could defend his duellist. A sword that became embedded in a shield could be bent with a twist of the shield, greatly impairing its user. To counter this, experienced duellists would wreck at least two of their opponent's three shields as fast as possible. This not only deprived the combatant of his best defence, but also of the services of his shield-bearer. Thus blows early in a fight were often directed at smashing shields rather than inflicting injury. An opponent who expected this might not be quick enough to defend an attempt at an early wound.

Unlike the Einvigi, a death in a Holmgang duel was not grounds for vengeance, and the family of the deceased had no redress for anything that happened in what was seen as a fair fight. Most duels did not end in death, of course, and allowed the participants to settle their dispute in a binding manner that, not coincidentally, displayed their courage and honour.

It was not permissible to retreat or dodge blows; they had to be taken on sword or shield in a suitably manly fashion. If a fighter put a foot off the cloak, there would be calls of 'flinch' or 'he yields ground', which suggested he was being a bit cowardly and needed to step up if he wanted to avoid ridicule. Leaving the cloak with both feet was grounds for derision, as it constituted fleeing a battle – better to take a blow than be seen a coward. Conversely, attacking vigorously and pressing forward attracted praise and would establish a man's reputation. Being wounded and having to pay a loser's fee to the winner was often seen as a small price compared to the word-fame to be won in such a duel.

The Holmgang duel was enshrined in law, and over time it became a matter of religious significance. Duelling sites were often located in sacred groves and other holy places, the duels accompanied by sacrifices and rituals to ward off any otherworldly influence that might unfairly affect the fight. It was well known, for example, that a berserker could cast a spell to blunt an opponent's sword, and protection against this sort of cheating was built into the duel formalities. The legal status of the Holmgang

ABOVE: This rune stone depicts two warriors engaging in what is probably an Einvigi duel, although there is no indication of what they are fighting about. The longship depicted below the fighters may or may not be significant to the quarrel.

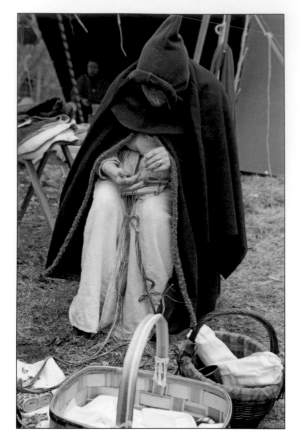

ABOVE: Re-enactments offer a fascinating insight into the day-to-day life of the Vikings. Modern observers are often surprised at how sophisticated their society was, and at the advanced techniques used to repair clothing, prepare food and carry out other domestic tasks.

duel was thus augmented by religious custom, with procedures taking on both social and spiritual significance.

Limits of the Law

Like many other aspects of Viking law, the formalization of the duel served to protect society against lawlessness and pointless violence. Feuding, raiding and so forth were acceptable, but without limiting factors there was a real danger that society would collapse. In a culture where the preferred form of justice was blood vengeance, the law served not so much as a deterrent as a guide to what was acceptable and what was not.

For example, theft was a serious crime and was considered deeply dishonourable, so much so that a court could condemn a thief to become a slave for his victim. Yet it was acceptable to attack a man's home, kill him and take his property if the assault took the form of a conventional raid. This was to some extent because a raid was seen as a challenge to combat, with the victor taking the spoils. The raid's target had a fair chance to defend himself and his property, and if he failed to be strong enough that was his fault, not that of the raiders.

In *Egil's Saga*, a band of raiders is captured but manages to escape, carrying off booty in the process. On the way back to their ships, the raiders decide that they are behaving dishonourably and have stolen their plunder rather than winning it in battle. Naturally, they go back and attack their target again, killing the defenders and burning their home. Honour is now satisfied and the goods they have taken can be considered fair booty.

It may seem strange to the modern observer that these raiders considered that pillage was fine as long as you killed people first, but taking property and leaving the owners alive was socially unacceptable. However, in their culture the distinction between stealing and taking by strength was a critically important one.

Notably, most of the Viking gods are honourable warriors, while the greatest villain in the universe is a trickster and a thief.

It was also unacceptable to harm women, both in law and social custom. In one of the sagas a chieftain orders his men to slay a woman and they refuse, as this would dishonour them. The concepts of honour and reputation were at the heart of Viking society and, unsurprisingly perhaps, found their way into laws. Those whose personal integrity did not stop them from undertaking certain acts would find themselves facing a law that enforced the same values.

Women were protected by custom and law, but were also bound by it. Women were not allowed to wear men's clothes, to bear arms or to cut their hair short. The law firmly established that women were noncombatants who must be left alone in return for not fighting or being in a position where they might be mistaken for a man in the heat of battle.

Women could also be raped, killed or taken as slaves during a raid, but the law protecting women applied uniformly to those within Viking society; those outside it could take their chances. Thus rape and murder were acceptable when directed at the women of people overseas, but if a Viking stead were to be burned in a local feud, the women and children were permitted to escape.

LEFT: Although it was unacceptable to attack women within Viking society, the rules were different during a raid against foreigners. Similarly, stealing property was dishonourable but killing a man for his goods was considered to be fair providing he had a chance to fight back.

4

VIKING SOCIETY

Social mobility was far more common in Viking society than in many other cultures. There were essentially three groups, with most people belonging to the class known as *Karls*. These were free people who owned some property and/or had useful skills.

Karls were farmers and landowners, merchants and craftsmen such as smiths and shipwrights (skilled carpenters and ship builders). A Karl could aspire to push himself up into the ruling class, the *Jarls*, by becoming wealthy and powerful.

Within the Karl class there were some loose social divisions. Landowners and well-off merchants were, in general, the most highly regarded of the Karls, with tenant farmers and craftsmen being of somewhat lesser status. Fishermen, farm hands and similar people employed by others were of relatively low status, but were still above freed slaves and vagrants.

Vagrants were free men, but unlike the rest of the Karl class they did not enjoy the full protection of the law. Indeed, it was legal to rob or even castrate a vagrant in Iceland. This was in part due to the importance of accountability in Icelandic Viking society. To be a proper member of society an individual had to be accountable, which meant that he had to have a permanent

OPPOSITE: **The return of a trading or raiding party was an anxious time. Men might have been killed during the expedition, or they might return empty-handed. A successful voyage was grounds for celebration as it could greatly increase the prosperity of the community.**

home where a summons to the Thing could be delivered. This was necessary to make him subject to the law, so an individual who had no home had a rather dubious legal status. The only people with less legal protection than vagrants were outlaws.

Money and property were not the only requirements to be a Jarl. Social status was also necessary – not something guaranteed by riches alone. A Jarl commanded the respect and loyalty of his supporters, but this was very much a two-way street. He was expected to protect the interests of his people and lead them in battle if necessary, and was to a great extent the guardian of their honour. A Jarl who was fair and reasonably generous, and who was seen to uphold the interests of his followers, would remain popular and perhaps even grow in power. One who was self-serving or indifferent might find that his followers' loyalty was transferred elsewhere.

Kings, Poets and Slaves

The most powerful members of the noble class were kings, although in the earlier part of the Viking Age they tended to be rulers of a fairly small area. Later on, great kingdoms arose but at the time of the first raids into Europe there were many small kingdoms, none of which were enormously powerful. The Vikings did not have a concept such as the 'divine right of rule'; they saw their Jarls and kings as merely rich, powerful and worthy men. Divine favour might help a man reach such status, but he ruled as a man, not a divine representative.

'TRUST NO MAN SO WELL THAT YOU TRUST NOT YOURSELF BETTER. MANY ARE UNFIT TO BE TRUSTED.'

In Iceland, the situation was somewhat different. There were no kings and indeed no Jarls, but the Godi fulfilled a similar function to the latter although they belonged to the Karl class. The Icelandic Vikings wanted no kings of their own but they did not apparently have much objection to others having them; Icelandic warriors could be found in the personal entourage of Scandinavian kings. Their adventures and the respect they earned in these posts contributed to raised status when they returned home, but again this was due to being an accomplished man and not association with a king.

Although not rich or powerful in quite the same way, poets were also part of the Jarl class. They were the keepers of history in a time when little was written down, and had the ability both to advise nobles and inspire people. Poets were held in very high regard for the knowledge they had and for what they could do. A skilled poet could enthral an audience with his tales, remind people of obscure facts and histories, and make them feel good about their society with tales of heroes, gods and ancestors.

Any Karl or Jarl could join the lower class of society if circumstances treated him badly. This group, known as *Thralls*, were slaves and bondsmen. Slaves were typically captured during raids or perhaps traded for, while bondsmen were those who could not pay their debts and had to work for their creditors until they were able to do so.

In some ways, slaves actually had more legal protection than vagrants. This may have reflected both their greater economic importance and the fact that their owners were properly accountable for the actions and behaviour, so the law was easier to enforce on a slave than on someone who might simply wander off into a different district.

Slaves were permitted to marry and to protect their family, taking vengeance against those who took advantage of their wives or daughters, and they could also own property. If a slave managed to garner enough wealth he could buy his freedom, although this made him a very low-status Karl and if he had no heirs his inheritance went to his former owner.

BELOW: **A romantic depiction of Rorik, who carved out a kingdom in Friesland. It is possible that his chosen weapon was a spiked club, but it is more likely that he was depicted this way to portray him as a noble savage.**

RIGHT: The harp was a
traditional instrument
of poets, who enjoyed
high status among the
upper echelons of Viking
society. They did not
rule, but were valuable
stores of knowledge that
could be called upon by
a king or Jarl.

RIGHT: The harp was a traditional instrument of poets, who enjoyed high status among the upper echelons of Viking society. They did not rule, but were valuable stores of knowledge that could be called upon by a king or Jarl.

Slaves were used for hard manual work, especially on farms, and were important to the economy as they could be forced to work very hard for next to no cost. In many areas they did the same work as hired farmhands, although their working conditions were worse. Sometimes conditions were bad enough, or slaves were sufficiently mistreated, that they revolted. To avoid this, it was considered wise not to have too many slaves despite the economic advantages to be gained from their cheap labour.

Extended Families

Large settlements were unusual in the Viking Age, and were mainly trade towns. Villages, as such, were also uncommon, with most people living in an extended family on a farmstead. The heart of this extended family was several married couples and their children. Usually most, if not all, of these couples had one member who was related to one or more of the other adults in the community. In addition to these couples there would be bondsmen or slaves, who might also have families.

Elders educated the children of a homestead in the skills they would need in adulthood. Sometimes boys would be sent to live with an expert in a field so that they could learn a high level of skills. Sometimes children were also fostered for various reasons.

The death of one or both parents was one obvious reason, while children from a large family might go to live with a couple whose own children had died. This was not uncommon – child mortality in this era has been estimated at about 50 per cent.

Children of high-status families were also sometimes fostered in the household of a social inferior, usually in return for financial support. Such arrangements created a sort of kinship between people who were not otherwise related and helped support the socially inferior family.

Fostering also saved some children who could not otherwise be supported by their parents, but some were rejected. This was usually due to deformity or obvious weakness, but at times parents who could not support a child would have no alternative but to place it outside and allow the elements to do their work.

A new child was considered accepted by its parents when the father named the child, sprinkling water on it, and the mother suckled it. Once this had been done the baby was a member of society and was protected by law. A child that had been accepted by its parents was recognized by the rest of society as the child of that couple and had inheritance rights.

BELOW: The Viking settlement at Jarlshof in the Shetland Islands was constructed on the site of earlier settlements going back to the Stone Age. Finds at Jarlshof make it one of the most important Norse archaeological sites in the British Isles.

Children were expected to work, but they were usually considered to be exempt from violence and permitted to flee a fight or raid unharmed. However, the definition of 'children' varies somewhat. In Iceland a boy of 12 was considered a man for the purposes of whether or not he could be a judge in court, and many girls were married at that age.

Marriage and Divorce

Marriage and the family structure were extremely important to the Vikings. Male and female roles were clearly defined and it was difficult for a single person to cope with the needs of day-to-day life. Thus if one partner died it was customary to remarry fairly soon. Marriage itself was seen as something akin to a business deal, and was often arranged between families. Indeed, there were laws prohibiting a man from creating poems of praise to a woman, and courting was in general discouraged.

Attempting to make a good marriage was a difficult business. If the matter was not approached correctly, the prospective bride's family might feel slighted and a feud could result; a rejected proposal could be seen as a grave insult to the prospective groom. Violence could result in other ways, too: in one of the Icelandic sagas, a father learns that his daughter is being courted with poems of praise and sends assassins after the suitor.

Assuming the prospective groom did not get himself killed or start a blood feud with the bride's family, the couple would be betrothed. This was essentially a binding promise of marriage, usually between the fathers of the prospective couple. Other representatives would serve if one or both fathers were dead. The betrothal took the form of a business arrangement, with the groom's father offering a bride-price at the time of betrothal and the bride's father paying a dowry upon marriage.

A marriage could be arranged without consulting the bride or groom, although trouble could result from this. The Icelandic

BELOW: **This cremation urn lid depicts the marriage of fertility deities, suggesting that the Vikings viewed life and death as parts of the same essential cycle. The concept of a new world after Ragnarök is another example of this belief.**

sagas cite numerous occasions where a bride is unhappy with the arrangements and refuses to marry, although of course this may have been in the interests of a good story. It is likely that most prospective couples accepted the arrangements and made the best of it, or made one another miserable for many years. It was in everyone's interests to arrange an acceptable marriage, however, so a certain amount of negotiation was likely in many cases.

The marriage itself was a fairly major occasion with feasting and celebrations that could last for days. Divorce, on the other hand, could be a fairly quick and easy business. Either of the couple could simply declare a divorce in front of witnesses. However, there were other complications. Both parties were entitled to half of their joint wealth, and determining who got what could be every bit as painful as it is today – with the added problem of angry relatives literally threatening blood vengeance.

Until she married, a woman was under the guardianship of her father, and upon marriage her new husband became her protector. Women were not permitted to participate in court as a witness or a judge, and could not speak at the Thing. They could, of course, exert influence over male members of their family who

ABOVE: This depiction of a Viking feast takes place in distinctly Classical surroundings rather than the more typical longhouse. Later artists attempted to re-imagine the Vikings to match Greek and Roman concepts popular at the time.

would speak on their behalf, and wielded power in subtle ways. In general, the woman was responsible for everything that went on in the home and the man for everything beyond it. But the man had to live in that house, and was therefore subject to the influence of his wife all the time he was at home.

Where a divorce was ruled to be the fault of the man, both bride-price and dowry reverted to the woman's family, and she also got half of the estate. The threat to declare a divorce could be a potent one, and even without such drastic measures a woman could control her household most of the time. Although women were not permitted on raiding or trade expeditions, they did handle the financial affairs of their family and were often indispensable to their partner. A widow would inherit her husband's estate and might, in the event where she chose not to marry again, be an important landowner in her own right.

In more general interactions between free people, the average Viking was expected to be fair, honest and generous – but not too generous. Among the maxims attributed to Odin are these:

No need to give too much to a man, a little can buy much thanks; with half a loaf and a tilted jug I often won me a friend.

Be a friend to your friend, match gift with gift; meet smiles with smiles, and lies with dissimulation.

Jarls and kings often used gift-giving as a system to reward and pay their followers. A man who fought well or acted faithfully in the service of his lord could expect a gift in return. The sagas and Viking histories record various instances of leaders gifting their men in recognition of good service, or offering a reward for whoever could perform a difficult task.

There was no negotiation of fee in these cases; the leader said that he would reward the man who accomplished his task and his men had faith that he would do as

BELOW: Gender roles were strictly defined in Viking society, with men as 'doers' and women as 'facilitators' who kept the family fed and clothed, and ran the household. A partnership of this sort created strengths that complemented one another, much as the two sets of gods represented fertility and war.

he said. A Jarl or king who failed to be suitably generous to his followers would find himself without support and also, in the eyes of many, without honour.

This was no more than an extension of the idea that a man should be fair and honest in his dealings with others. Loyalty was a two-way street in the Viking Age – a Karl who gave his loyalty to a Jarl had a right to expect something in return, and failure to uphold this unspoken but very real bargain could have fatal consequences. This was, after all, an age in which blood vengeance was the preferred form of justice, and feuds could result from a minor slight.

Clothing

Even those that took part in the raids and exploration voyages that made the Vikings famous were not full-time warriors. Most were farmers or landowners, spending much of their year running their estate or working at their craft. A Viking who survived childhood might expect to live 40-odd years or so; only a small percentage of the population survived past 60, but of those who did, some lived to a great age. There are records of individuals aged 80 or more.

One requirement for a long life in conditions that could be cold and harsh was suitable clothing. The style of clothing worn by Vikings varied slightly over time and in different areas, but was broadly similar to that of other 'barbarian' people of Germanic origin in northern Europe. This is hardly surprising; these people all had similar materials to work with and were trying to meet the same basic needs of warmth and durability.

'THE LONGER THE VENGEANCE IS DRAWN OUT, THE MORE SATISFYING IT WILL BE.'

The construction of Viking clothes was fairly sophisticated, with cloth woven on a loom and then cut into the parts necessary to make a garment. Animal products such as furs were used wherever they were available. Garments, especially, were often made from many pieces and were cleverly sewn together. This was a complex process but produced little waste. The result was an image that has become familiar and is reasonably accurate –

men dressed in trousers and a long tunic, with a woollen cloak and probably a hat, and wearing leather shoes. This image, with local variations, applies to 'barbarian' peoples across much of Europe and western Asia.

Viking clothing used few complex parts like pockets or a fly, and few fasteners. Drawstrings, pins and the occasional button sufficed to keep everything in place. If this was inconvenient when nature called, it did make clothing simpler to make and probably contributed to durability. Clothing had to fit reasonably well but still permit freedom of movement; tight clothing was considered to be an affectation of snappy dressers. Using excessive amounts of cloth was another affectation, but one perhaps less questionable. A rich man's tunic would be longer than normal, reaching all the way to his knees, while his poorer neighbour might have one that ended at mid thigh.

> 'OFTEN A MAN BECOMES BRAVE IN DIRE STRAIGHTS, WHO IS NOT BRAVE MOST OTHER TIMES.'

There is evidence from the sagas that early in the Viking period men did not wear undergarments, but later tales include a surprising number of incidents of heroes running around in their underwear for various reasons. Sleepwear is also definitely not present in some stories but is worn in others; this may have been nothing more than personal preference, or styles may have changed over time.

Underpants, when they were worn, were probably knee-length trousers secured with a drawstring. They would usually have been made from wool, although for richer Vikings linen was preferable as it was more comfortable. An undershirt or undertunic, sometimes of linen, was also worn, and many Vikings who did not have trousers that included foot coverings used socks.

Viking trouser designs varied considerably. As already noted, some included foot coverings and some did not. Some were secured by a drawstring, others had belt loops or even both, and some had straps that ran under the foot to prevent trousers riding up. Additional protection for the lower legs was offered by wrapping strips of cloth around the leg, spiralling down from the knee to the foot. This was uncommon in Iceland and western Viking lands, but further east leg protection of this form was used at times.

Viking belts were fairly narrow but served several useful purposes. As well as holding up the trousers they were also used to carry a pouch and other small items, such as a knife. With no pockets in Viking clothing, the belt pouch was one of the few ways any object could be carried without tying up a hand that might be needed for work or fighting.

The main upper-body garment was a long-sleeved tunic that slipped over the head and was sometimes secured at the neck by a single button. This was made of wool and decorated to varying degrees depending on the wealth of the owner. A cloak was worn for additional warmth, secured with a pin.

Hats generally took the form of a simple cap formed from triangular pieces of cloth. Other designs of hat included fur caps, with or without ear flaps, and a sort of hood known as a *hottr*, which was caped and covered the shoulders to deflect rain and snow.

Shoes were typically high, coming up over the ankle, but were not boots as such. They were fastened with laces or toggles, and were not always very secure. Viking heroes occasionally lose their shoes mid-battle in the sagas – Ogmund loses both of his in the snow at one point, but is lucky to have a loyal friend to protect him while he sorts the problem out.

Women wore an under-dress that reached to the ground and was secured at the neck by a brooch, and either a full over-dress or an apron-skirt, which hung from the shoulders on straps. A cloak was also worn for warmth, and head-coverings were common. These varied from a simple cloth to a variety of hats. Shoes were the same as those worn by men.

Longhouses

Another requirement for survival in the hard Viking lands was a warm and solid place to live. The typical Viking home was a longhouse inhabited by an extended family. A farmstead might have one or perhaps two longhouses. Early in the Viking Age,

BELOW: **Viking clothing was simple in appearance but was cleverly made to use the least material possible. There were few fasteners: a button and a pin or two, plus a belt.**

the longhouse was the only building and served for all functions – living, storage and working at crafts – but later in the era it became more common to have additional outbuildings such as workshops or storage sheds.

Buildings were constructed with a variety of materials, including stone, wood and turf or wattle and daub, and in some cases wooden walls were braced with iron bands. Many buildings had walls that bowed outwards at the centre of the long axis, creating a wider central space. This was less pronounced in many larger buildings, where the whole space could be wide enough for use. Beams resting on a double row of posts supported the roof, which ensured that the walls were not pushed outward by the weight of the roof and contributed greatly to the structural integrity of the longhouse.

The inside was subdivided into rooms, with the central space between the roof supports serving as a corridor and also the site of the fire in most longhouses. The fire sat in a pit or, occasionally, a stone hearth. The latter, if it were present, might contain a space for use as an oven. There were rarely any windows in a longhouse.

BELOW: Longhouses were built around a wooden frame, over which walls of wood or perhaps wattle and daub were constructed. Some houses used iron strips to support and reinforce the frame. The weight of the roof rested on poles within the house rather than on the walls.

LEFT: Most longhouses were well lit during daytime, with light coming in through smokeholes and the open door. At night, the fire and a few oil lamps provided sufficient illumination. Windows were rare, although there are accounts of some longhouses having them.

Smokeholes allowed additional light into the building as well as permitting smoke from the fire to escape. They could also allow cold draughts into the building, so a good balance had to be struck between enough holes for ventilation and too many for warmth. The positioning of smokeholes was an important matter; a longhouse with incorrectly placed holes would fill up with smoke and be unpleasant to remain in at best.

There are mentions in some sagas of longhouses with lofts as sleeping chambers, and some surviving buildings seem to have them. However, such an arrangement might offer the worst of all worlds -- smoke that had not yet escaped from the building would make the space unpleasant to be in, and it would probably be cold due to draughts entering through the smokeholes.

In daytime during warmer conditions, the door of a longhouse could be left open to let in light. Doors were made of wood and hung on hinges of metal or wood. Some longhouses had lockable doors, but in all probability they were not locked very often. A longhouse would not stand empty unless it had been abandoned – there would always be people moving in and out during the day, or working within, and at night it was the sleeping quarters for the entire household. Any intruder willing to take on a building full of angry Vikings was not likely to be stopped by even the most firmly secured door.

ABOVE: The reconstructed longhouse and outbuildings at L'Anse aux Meadows gives an indication of the character of Viking buildings – low, sturdy and functional. Re-enactors have found that the longhouse is a warm and generally quite pleasant place to live.

Furniture within the longhouse was fairly minimal. The head of the household usually had a bed-closet and a high chair to mark his status, while everyone else used long benches that were part of the building. These ran the length of the longhouse and were constructed of wood or earth topped with wood. They provided seating for work and meals, and served as beds for the household at night.

Not all households had tables. Those that did used a trestle design that could be stored when not in use. They may have been suspended from the roof beams to keep them out of the way, or simply placed to one side. There was also often a chest for the householder's valuables, which might be very soundly constructed with iron reinforcement and a sturdy lock. Other chests might be used to store lesser items, and could serve as impromptu seating at other times. Those who had them might use stools or, occasionally, chairs, but most members of the household made do with the benches.

Outbuildings were generally of simpler construction, often with a sunken floor. This made construction easier, as lower walls were needed, and such buildings could be quickly constructed as necessary. They were used for storage and as working areas, and may have been used to house Thralls (bondsmen and slaves) who were not permitted to live in the longhouse.

Farmsteads

Life was hard in the farmsteads, but perhaps better than elsewhere. Trading towns were less healthy places to be, with poor sanitation and larger numbers of people in close proximity to one another than the norm. Disease was more common in the towns than the farmsteads, where most individuals worked outdoors in cold conditions but probably ate fairly well, contributing to good health overall. The typical diet for these people depended on their location but included cereal crops and vegetables, plus dairy products, meat and fish.

The most important animals on a farm were cattle, to the point where the same word was used for cattle and for money, and wealth was often measured in terms of herd size. Cattle-farming practices were somewhat similar to those used today, inasmuch as most bulls were slaughtered for food in the autumn or sacrificed to the gods, with only a small proportion kept for breeding purposes.

Beef was commonly eaten in times of prosperity, but a hard winter could seriously reduce the size of a herd. Where fodder was in short supply, preference was given to milk cows, which were also more likely to be sheltered indoors in the winter months. Sheep were also extensively herded for their wool as well as meat and sometimes milk, and like most of the cattle sheep were generally allowed to wander and graze as they pleased. At the beginning of winter they would be rounded up and brought closer to the stead, even if they were not to be penned indoors.

BELOW: The Vikings in general enjoyed a varied diet with plenty of meat prepared in a variety of ways. Stew and bread was a common meal, but could be kept interesting by using a range of seasonings available.

Many farms also had goats and pigs, although the latter proved so troublesome to the Icelandic settlers that laws were passed to try to limit the amount of damage done by wandering pigs. Horsemeat was also eaten, at least until the coming of Christianity to the Viking world, and horses were widely used as transport and draft animals alongside oxen. The horse herds of the Swedes, in particular, were very good, and many warriors rode into battle before the beginning of the Viking Age. The practice of fighting on foot became prevalent later, but this did not stop some warriors at least riding to the site of a battle.

Hunting, Eating and Drinking

Meat came from farm animals and was also hunted, while fish were caught with both line and net. Some communities supplemented their diet with whale meat, although this was probably more opportunistic than deliberate. It has been suggested that Viking ships attempted to drive whales ashore, but it is more likely that any beached whales got there for other reasons and were then butchered for food.

BELOW: **This scoop and milk skimmer are typical of the tools found in a Viking kitchen. A wide variety of sophisticated kitchen utensils were available, many of which used non-metal materials that were much cheaper to obtain.**

The common image of spit-roasted animals probably occurred only at feasts, perhaps at the beginning of winter when many animals were slaughtered to make sure there was enough fodder for the remainder. More commonly, food was stewed or boiled in a cauldron. Stews have the advantage that they can be made with almost anything, enabling the household to use up whatever was available. A stew can feed a variable number of people as well, especially if plentiful bread is available, and is thus more practical for day-to-day sustenance than a purpose-made meal.

A bowl of stew and bread was a far more likely prospect than a spit-roasted ox, except at feast times. Bread was unleavened and probably prepared especially for each meal, of which there were usually two a day, plus breakfast. Meals were served at midmorning and in the evening, and were usually eaten by the whole household together. Most households had trestle tables that could be stored when not in use, and long benches where the extended family sat to eat.

Although there will have been times when food was in short supply and everyone had to make do with what they could get, for the most part Viking cuisine was reasonably complex. Various spices and flavourings were available, although the only known sweetener was honey. Stews were eaten with a spoon from a bowl, with more solid foods served on wooden trenchers. Individuals possessed a knife, which was a general-purpose tool as well as an eating utensil, and was used for most meals.

Although Vikings are famously depicted as drinking mead, ale was more common. Beer and mead were produced, but the everyday drink for adults and children alike was ale. This may make the Vikings seem like a mob of howling drunks but the alcohol content of ale was important for health reasons. Even in a rural setting, away from the crowded trade towns, water was not always safe to drink. Human and animal waste could get into any well or stream, and contamination could be picked up during storage. The alcohol in ale killed bacteria just as the heat applied to water used in cooking did, making ale much safer to drink than water.

Food was typically preserved by smoking or allowing the cold, dry air to dry out meat and fish, enabling stores to be put aside for the winter months, augmented by hunting, fishing and slaughtering the occasional farm animal. There is little evidence to suggest that the Vikings were underfed or suffered from

ABOVE: A common method of preserving fish was air drying, taking advantage of the cold and dry conditions. As an alternative, meat or fish could be smoked by hanging it from the roof beams above a fire pit.

nutritional deficiencies, so an adequate supply of food must have been available year-round, at least most of the time.

Sickness, Hygiene and Grooming

Various cures were available for those who did fall ill. Some were based on magic, but the healing properties of several herbs were clearly understood. The art of setting broken bones was well known, and physical injuries could be treated by methods that would be familiar today: bandages, splints and the need to keep a wound clean. Cauterization was used to deal with serious bleeding, and there is evidence that surgery was used with at least occasional success.

Those who were wounded or otherwise injured were expected to be stoic about their pain and not make a fuss. Indeed, bearing the pain of injuries was seen as manly and admirable, such as the tale of a warrior with a severely damaged foot who announced that 'one does not limp when both legs are the same length'.

There is archaeological evidence that some warriors suffered extremely serious injuries in combat and survived them; some skeletons have what are obviously old, healed wounds on them. Survival rates in battle may have been improved by elementary first aid training given to warriors. There are accounts of leaders calling a brief truce to allow the men of both sides to tend their bleeding wounds before attempting to inflict further injuries on one another.

Although the Vikings have been depicted as unwashed savages, personal hygiene played a large part in their culture. Combs are very common archaeological finds, and are often hand crafted with fine teeth and decoration. The sagas suggest that although a man's clothing, shoes and horse might be in poor condition, he should be 'washed and combed' when appearing before the assembly. Other sagas suggest that a measure of personal grooming was as normal in the morning as having something to eat. Arab writers speak of the Vikings washing their faces every morning, and the mountain of Helgafjell was considered so holy that one could not look in its direction without washing the face first.

BELOW: Drinking horns were sometimes used, although more practical vessels were also available. It is possible that horns were used for ceremonial or festive occasions; the Eddas and sagas tell of occasions where horns are used for drinking.

LEFT: **A comb was an important possession. Icelandic law stated that it was acceptable to appear at the Thing in old and patched clothes as long as the beard and hair were combed.**

Where hot springs existed, they were used for bathing on a regular basis. Bath-houses were constructed to take advantage of these conditions. But even where hot water was not naturally occurring, Vikings were expected to wash and clean themselves. Some longhouses seem to have had a room similar to a sauna, and there are records of Anglo-Saxon women preferring Norse men to their own because they were cleaner.

Icelandic law lists several grave offences revolving around trying to disgrace or humiliate someone by throwing dirt at him or pushing him into it, and it was viewed very seriously. This surely would not be the case among a bunch of filthy savages, and provides additional evidence that the Vikings greatly valued personal hygiene and their appearance in general.

Men typically wore beards, but were expected to keep them presentable. Cutting and washing hair was a task performed by women and may have taken on a ritual significance. The sagas record instances of heroes having their hair cut and washed before taking on a difficult task, and in his saga Viglundur promises Ketilrirour that he will not permit anyone else to perform this task for him while she lives. This suggests a level of intimacy was at least sometimes associated with hair-dressing.

Harald Fine-Hair, eventual king of Norway, is said to have vowed not to have his hair cut or washed until he had gained control over his kingdom. This task took a decade to complete, and it was not until afterwards that Harald gained his honorific. In this case it was Harald's friend Rognvald Eysteinsson who performed the haircut. Rognvald founded the Earldom of Orkney and was possibly the father of Rollo, first Viking leader in Normandy. He was an important and powerful man, and in this case the hair-cutting probably indicates trust and friendship as well as social esteem – Rognvald performed the haircut that would only be permitted when Harald was king of Norway.

RIGHT: **The runes consisted of straight strokes and were easy to carve or chisel into stone or wood. Most Vikings could read the runes and sent one another messages on rune-sticks.**

Whatever the circumstances, he did a good job and Harald was henceforth renowned for the standard of his personal grooming.

Viking Literacy

As well as general cleanliness, literacy was fairly common. The Vikings used a runic alphabet, in which each character was composed of straight lines. This made inscriptions relatively easy to chisel into wood or stone, and messages were often sent on rune-sticks. Wax writing tablets were also used, providing a reusable medium for practice or short-term notes.

There was no absolute convention on how the runes were written down. They could be written to read in either direction, with alternate lines often zig-zagging in this manner. Each rune could also represent several different sounds, so meaning had to be built from context and the surrounding runes. Much of the Vikings' history and law was orally recorded rather than written down; rune-sticks were generally used for short messages and there are few surviving major bodies of writing from the pre-Christian era.

This suggests that runic writing was thought to be appropriate for communications, even important ones, but that for long-term information storage the minds of men were considered superior. Most people could read and write the runes, but few were talented enough to become a Lawspeaker or a poet. It is for this reason that many of the Viking sagas and mythology did not come to be written down until much later, and in places may have become corrupted by later individuals' patterns of thought.

'NEVER BREAK THE PEACE WHICH GOOD AND TRUE MEN MAKE BETWEEN YOU AND OTHERS.'

Scourge of Civilization

The common image of the Viking as some sort of homicidal lunatic, leaping out of a longship to destroy everything he sets eyes upon, is thus shown as being somewhat erroneous. He was not an untutored savage with a filthy, matted beard; he could read messages on a rune-stick and wore well-made clothes that he took care of by washing them once a week. He also washed himself and combed his beard. He was not a professional robber and murderer – he was probably a householder or a craftsman, with a well-constructed farm or home to go back to. Nor was he the product of a howling wilderness filled with desperate savages; he came from a well-ordered and relatively civilized society ruled by law to create a stable social order.

And yet he did leap out of a longship into the surf, to rush ashore and pillage as he pleased. He slew anyone who tried to stop him and boasted about his deeds afterwards. He did these things for reasons that made perfect sense to him and his peers. Economic, social and religious factors made him who and what he was, and to him the savagery of the raid was just one facet of his complex and even quite sophisticated lifestyle.

To his victims, however, he was the scourge of civilization and the enemy of God. Within just a few years of the Lindisfarne raid it would seem that no coast was safe from these terrible Northmen, and their raids would reach far inland too. The 'fury of the Northmen' quote may be hard to attribute to an original source, but it does accurately express the sentiment of the time.

5

THE EARLY RAIDS

The history of the Vikings is a complex tale and one that is hard to break into simple 'eras'. There was no clearly defined period of raiding followed by a period of settlement and then one of large kingdoms; raiding, settlement and empire building went on throughout the Viking Age.

It is possible to discern a change in the way the Vikings, in the broadest sense, operated over time. In the early part of the Viking Age expeditions set out from their homes in Scandinavia to raid, explore and trade, returning home afterwards. Later, the Vikings took land and created kingdoms. There is no single point where raiding stopped – it never did – and there was always some settlement going on as well as colonization by other means. This was mainly by way of migration, whereby some Vikings left traditionally Viking lands and joined existing societies, and in some cases ended up becoming an elite military class or even the rulers of this society.

It is thus easier to comprehend the story of the Vikings in terms of activity – raiding, exploring or settling – than in terms of a strict chronology. At any given moment, raiding might be

OPPOSITE: **Viking ship design changed remarkably little throughout the era. Small and relatively simple, these vessels could brave the North Atlantic yet were light enough to portage over rapids in the great rivers of Europe and Russia.**

the norm in one area, while in another region relatively peaceful settlement was taking place. Throughout their long history the way other societies viewed the Vikings gradually changed, from fearsome foreigners to (equally fearsome, perhaps) neighbours.

This change was not uniform in location nor over time, and nor was it complete, but the trend is clearly identifiable. By the end of the Viking Age, the Norsemen would be very much a part of the European political landscape, but in 793 AD they were distant foreigners about whom little was known. Their arrival on the world stage was dramatic and bloody, but the true implications would not become clear for many years. When that first raiding party stormed up the beach at Lindisfarne, nobody could have predicted how much the world was about to change.

BELOW: Early raids were small, with just a handful of ships involved, but the scale quickly grew until dozens and eventually hundreds of ships, carrying thousands of warriors, might be involved.

Booty and Plunder

Sea-raiding was nothing new to the Vikings in 793 AD, although recent advances in ship-building had increased the reach of traders and raiding parties. The economics of the raid were well known: it had to produce sufficient booty to justify the time spent away from farms and homesteads or at least result in increased fame, which had a different but equally palpable worth.

LEFT: Monasteries were prime targets for raiding. Lightly defended and often remote, they were low-risk objectives that were made even more attractive by the concentration of wealth to be found there.

In the longer term, raids and other expeditions had to pay for the building and maintenance of ships as well as weapons and equipment. Booty had to be of the low-bulk/high-value sort, as space in the Vikings' ships was rather limited. Also, the target could not be too well defended. A decent fight was necessary for word-fame and a chance to enter Valhol, and also to make the raid worthy of the name rather than being simple thievery. But if the defenders were too strong, or help arrived too quickly, then the Vikings might be driven off without taking any plunder.

Also, while there might be exceptions, most Vikings were not necessarily in a hurry to enter Valhol. A good life, enjoying the riches garnered in successful raids, was desirable; entry to Valhol would happen when it was fated, so why not have a good time in Midgard first? Thus the Vikings were not interested in suicide attacks or targets where they might still be struggling to get through the fortifications when reinforcements arrived to help the defenders.

All these factors greatly influenced the choice of targets. Ideally, they were fairly remote and beyond immediate assistance, defended lightly and not heavily fortified. Large settlements were likely to be able to muster a sizable force to resist raiders, so the target must not be too populous. Farms and small communities would yield a few valuables but high-value goods were to be found in high-value targets such as the homes of nobles or other leaders. Of course, these were likely to be well defended and were usually situated in or near a reasonably large settlement.

Small wonder, then, that coastal churches and monasteries were seen as ideal targets. Their location offered the Vikings quick access and an easy retirement with their booty. Many holy places were deliberately sited in remote locations, ensuring that they were beyond assistance within the duration of a typical raid.

> 'THERE ARE FEW MORE CERTAIN TOKENS OF ILL THAN NOT TO KNOW HOW TO ACCEPT THE GOOD.'

Religious buildings were possibly the highest-value targets available. The early Church was wealthy, with large quantities of gold and other valuables stored or in use at its buildings. More precious materials were used to decorate religious objects and the building itself. This ostentatious wealth was enough to make a prospective raider drool in anticipation.

The Lindisfarne Raid

Lindisfarne, situated on an island off the northeastern coast of England, was a perfect target for a raid. So perfect, in fact, that in hindsight Lindisfarne is the obvious choice for raiders coming across the North Sea. Yet at the time there was no real reason to suspect that an attack was likely or even possible. Apart from anything else an attack on a holy place of this sort was an assault on the socially and politically powerful church and an affront to God. Surely nobody would dare plunder a monastery?

However, the Vikings were not afraid of the Christian God – they had a whole pantheon of powerful gods of their own – or of the society that the Church was part of. In the eyes of the Church they were attacking God's own house, but in their own minds the Lindisfarne raid was more akin to a bank job. There was plunder to be had, the defenders were too weak to keep their possessions and conditions were perfect for a quick in-and-out raid.

Had the Lindisfarne raid gone badly awry, history might have been somewhat different. Perhaps the Vikings might have preferred to trade more and raid less. But in the event the expedition was an enormous success. Viking ships ran up onto the beach and disgorged warriors who slew with abandon. They entered the holy places and took whatever they could carry away, killing anyone who tried to stop them and many who were simply not quick enough to flee. Some of the monks were deliberately murdered by drowning or put to the sword, even though they were not fighting back, while others were taken as slaves.

The Lindisfarne raid proved that the concept was sound, and soon expeditions were planned against other coastal targets. At first the same stretch of coast was attacked; Jarrow and Wearmouth were raided in 794 AD. Then the attacks began farther afield – by 800 AD Viking ships were raiding targets from the isle of Iona to the southwest coast of France, and had also struck islands off the coast of Ireland.

Raids against Ireland began in 795 AD and were probably carried out by fairly small bands at first. They struck islands rather than the mainland for reasons connected with the sea – it made the target accessible to the longships and would slow down an organized response. The pattern in Ireland was not very different from elsewhere – coastal communities and monasteries were raided just like everywhere else – but in Ireland the reaction was somewhat different.

LEFT: The cutting down of a holy man is central to this depiction of a raid on a settlement in Ireland, but to the warriors involved there was nothing special about killing a monk or priest. The goal was plunder, and anyone in the way was liable to become a victim.

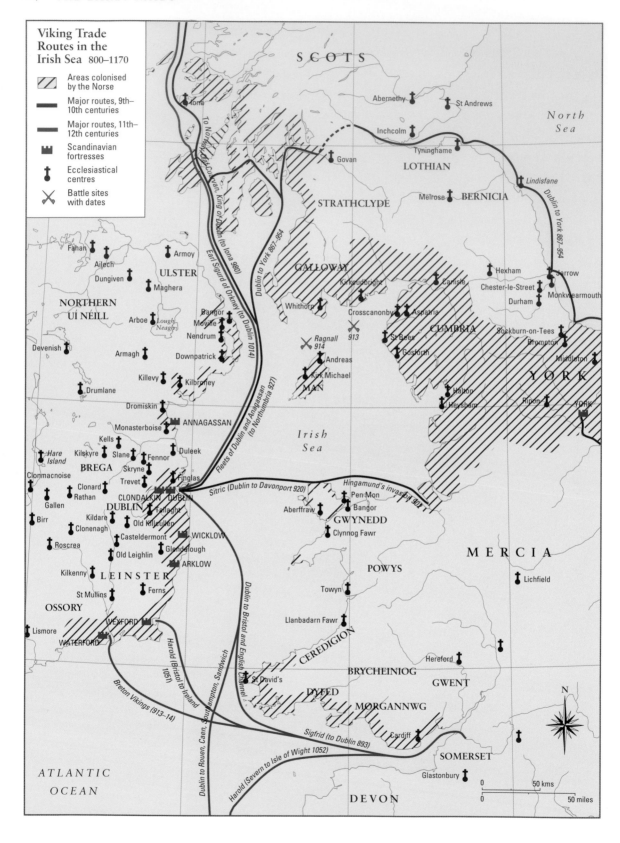

Viking Trade Routes in the Irish Sea 800–1170

Areas colonised by the Norse

Major routes, 9th–10th centuries

Major routes, 11th–12th centuries

Scandinavian fortresses

Ecclesiastical centres

Battle sites with dates

SCOTS

North Sea

Abernethy

St Andrews

Inchcolm

To Norway via Cumbran, King of Dublin (to Iona 980)

Govan

Tyninghame

LOTHIAN

Earl Sigurd of Orkney (to Dublin 1014)

Dublin to York 867–954

Lindisfane

STRATHCLYDE

Mélrose

BERNICIA

Fahan

Armoy

Hexham

Jarrow

Ailech

GALLOWAY

Carlisle

Chester-le-Street

Monkwearmouth

Dungiven

ULSTER

Kirkcudbright

Aspatria

Durham

Maghera

Whithorn

Crosscanonby

St Bees

Stockburn-on-Tees

NORTHERN
UI NEILL

Arboe

Lough
Neagh

Bangor

Moville

Nendrum

Ragnall
914

913

Andreas

Gosforth

CUMBRIA

Brompton

Devenish

Armagh

Downpatrick

Kirk Michael

Middleton

Killevy

MAN

YORK

Kilbroney

Halton

Drumlane

Heysham

Dromiskin

Monasterboise

ANNAGASSAN

Irish
Sea

Ripon

YORK

Kells

Fleets of Dublin and Anagassan (to Northumbria 927)

Hare
Island

Kilskyre

Slane

Fennor

Duleek

BREGA

Skryne

Trevet

Finglas

Clonmacnoise

Clonard

Rathan

CLONDALKIN   DUBLIN

Sitric (Dublin to Davonport 920)

Hingamund's invasion 902

Gallen

Kildare

DUBLIN

Tallaght

Old Killcullen

Aberffraw

Pen-Mon

Bangor

Birr

Clonenagh

Casteldermont

WICKLOW

GWYNEDD

Roscrea

Old Leighlin

Glendalough

ARKLOW

Clynnog Fawr

MERCIA

Kilkenny

LEINSTER

Ferns

POWYS

Lichfield

St Mullins

Towyn

OSSORY

Lismore

WEXFORD

WATERFORD

Harold (Bristol to Ireland) 1051

Dublin to Bristol and English Channel

Llanbadarn Fawr

CEREDIGION

St David's

Hereford

BRYCHEINIOG

GWENT

Breton Vikings (913–14)

Dublin to Rouen, Caen, Southampton, Sandwich

DYFED

MORGANNWG

Cardiff

Sigfrid (to Dublin 893)

Harold (Severn to Isle of Wight 1052)

SOMERSET

ATLANTIC
OCEAN

Glastonbury

DEVON

N

0   50 kms

0   50 miles

The monasteries of Ireland were embroiled in local politics and attacks upon them were not unknown. Burning the monastery of an enemy was sometimes the goal of tribal conflicts in Ireland. Churchmen would join in the raids and were probably used to fighting even if they did not actively train for it. Raiding for cattle and plunder were also social institutions in Ireland, so the depredations of the Vikings were not a great surprise to the local population.

Of all the places targeted by Viking raids, Lindisfarne was the most shocking, and not only because it was the first. In fact, Viking parties might have raided other holy places before Lindisfarne, but this was the first major site to be struck. Lindisfarne was a major centre for Christianity in England, and was the resting-place for Saint Bede. It had been a holy site since the 630s AD and if anywhere deserved the protection of God it was the monastery at Lindisfarne.

It was not uncommon at the time to assume that if disaster befell it was somehow deserved. It was strongly suggested that the sacking of Lindisfarne was divine retribution for a lack of piety, or insufficient generosity to the Church, or one of a wide range of activities – including adultery, fornication, avarice, incest and preoccupation with worldly luxury. The English were admonished by foreign religious figures to clean up their act; the raids would presumably stop when Englishmen were once again in favour with the Lord.

Strike at Will

Whether or not piety in England increased, the raids did not stop. Any coastal location was subject to raiding, and rivers provided the Viking ships with a means to reach targets that might have seemed far inland. The raiders did not like to go far from their ships, however, so settlements located at a distance from navigable waterways remained safe for the time being. However, the design of the ships, which permitted them to land on any beach and to manoeuvre under oars in tight spaces, enabled the Vikings to strike more or less at will.

ABOVE: Abbot Alcuin sent this letter of support for the survivors of the Lindisfarne raid. He commiserated but also admonished the monks to work harder at the Lord's work, suggesting that the raids would stop when they displayed sufficient piety.

OPPOSITE: When trade was likely to be more profitable than plundering, the Vikings were traders. Their ships followed much the same routes whether they intended commerce or violence.

ABOVE: **This 1950s
illustration of a
Viking raid portrays
the violence and looting
well enough, although
there are several
inaccuracies. The idea
of horned helmets,
for one, has long since
been discredited.**

Factors that might alter the target of a raid included wind and tide. During the voyage across the North Sea, Viking ships might be swept somewhat north or south of their intended path by weather conditions. It was of course entirely feasible to sail up or down the coast looking for the original objective, but often an alternative target would present itself. The Vikings were not making war so damaging a specific target was not really necessary. All that mattered was coming home with the proceeds to make the trip worthwhile.

Booty from a raid was shared out equally, subject to certain rules. The assumption was that every man who took part in a raid played his part and deserved a share of what the group as a whole earned. There were exceptions: a man seen to be in too much of a hurry to get back aboard the longships would forfeit his share if he left behind others who were still fighting. Since such a circumstance implied cowardice, accusing a man of doing so was more than a financial matter. It was a challenge to his honour and grounds for a duel or even blood feud.

Hostages and Brides

Although the carrying-off of material plunder was certainly profitable, there were other ways to make money by raiding. One was to take prisoners to be sold as slaves. It is possible to view these unfortunates as human booty, as they became property to be used or sold just like any other object. However, potential slaves had to be fed on the journey home and might be troublesome if they felt they had nothing to lose. To be valuable, a slave had to be able-bodied or perhaps have some useful skill. However, there was another way to make a profit from people taken in a raid: hostages.

The practice of hostage-taking may well have predated the Lindisfarne raid, but certainly within a few years it had become a lucrative business. Rather than transport potential slaves home, hostages could be ransomed back almost immediately after a raid, or taken to a settlement for holding until the ransom was paid. Hostages did not need to be good workers; all that mattered was that someone cared enough about them to pay a ransom. Naturally, individuals of economic significance or of personal importance to those who had wealth were the best prospects for raising a ransom.

Hostage-taking had another advantage. The market could theoretically become saturated with slaves, forcing the price down, and the loss of workers would weaken the economy of the raid target. On a one-off raid this was of little consequence but, in the longer term, less prosperous targets offered reduced booty. It was thus good business to ransom hostages back to their communities. There, they could go back to work rebuilding the local economy and make a future raid worthwhile. The same individuals could even be ransomed more than once.

Some targets were worth hitting repeatedly. The island monastery Noirmoutier was attacked every year until it was finally abandoned, while the coastal trading towns of Frisia were lucrative targets even if raided on several occasions.

Raids were not always simply about booty and pillage. There are cases in the sagas of warriors who wanted fame and a test

LEFT: The original defences at Noirmoutier were built to protect against Viking raids, and were not wholly successful. This later keep was built on the same site in the twelfth century.

of their manliness, but were not concerned about gold. Others raided only those who they felt deserved it, such as bands of outlaws or rival raiders. However, for the most part the Vikings were concerned with personal gain and prestige, and sometimes raided to capture a bride. Among the most notable of these incidents was the attack by Gudrod the Hunting-King on the kingdom of Agdir.

At the time, there were many small kingdoms in the Viking world, and Gudrod sought to increase his power by marrying the daughter of King Harald Red-Beard of Agdir. When his overtures were rebuffed, Gudrod took a more direct approach. He landed a force in Agdir, killed Harald and his son in battle, and kidnapped himself a royal bride. She bore him a son, known as Halfdan the Black, and eventually had her husband killed before returning home. Halfdan duly became King of Agdir and inherited half of his father's kingdom as well, becoming the powerful overlord that his father had sought to be.

BELOW: **Viking traders and raiding parties would sail wherever there was sea, and landed on any shore they found. Expeditions penetrated into the Mediterranean at least as far as Italy, as depicted here.**

The murder of Gudrod took place, if the sagas are to be believed, around 840 AD, and at this time the nature of Viking raids was changing. In the early years it was common for raiding parties to consist of a single ship or perhaps up to three. This number began to increase rapidly, and by 850 AD it was common to see fleets of 300 ships setting off on a large-scale raid.

Another major change took place around this time. In 843 AD a Viking raiding party wintered in Europe for the first time, rather than sailing home to Scandinavia. This led naturally to settlement, and soon the small Viking outposts in Aquitaine and elsewhere began to grow. A foray into the Mediterranean in 844 AD was repulsed after several cities had been attacked, but others followed and reached North Africa and even Italy.

Striking Inland

The Vikings also began to strike further inland, sometimes using horses, and conducted organized campaigns from forward bases established for the purpose. Inland raids, as opposed to strikes against islands and coastal towns, began in Ireland in 836 AD, and in 852 AD the first Vikings wintered on English soil.

In the 850s, a large raiding force known as the Great Army, possibly led by Ragnar Lodbrok, emerged in Europe. This force attacked Paris in 845 AD and launched a series of major raids throughout France, sacking some towns repeatedly. The size of this force is unclear but was probably around several thousand men, requiring hundreds of ships.

After campaigning in France, the Great Army moved to England, landing in East Anglia in 865 AD. The sagas suggest that the invasion was triggered by the death in battle of Ragnar Lodbrok and was led by his sons, but not all of the evidence is clear. According to legend, Ragnar launched an expedition against Northumbria that failed.

'TO TAKE UP GREAT RESOLUTIONS, AND THEN TO LAY THEM ASIDE, ONLY ENDS IN DISHONOR.'

It is not clear whether the Ragnar that landed in Northumbria was the same one who attacked Paris 20 years before, but it does seem likely that this Ragnar was advancing in years and was in danger of being eclipsed by the glory that his sons were winning.

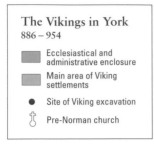

The Vikings in York
886 – 954

Ecclesiastical and administrative enclosure

Main area of Viking settlements

● Site of Viking excavation

☦ Pre-Norman church

RIGHT: **The naturally defensible position of York made it an ideal stronghold when reinforced with formidable walls. The Vikings took advantage of earlier fortification work and added some sections of their own.**

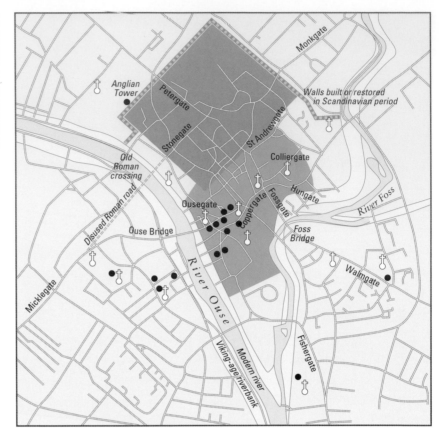

Lodbrok means 'hairy-breeks', a name derived from the special trousers his wife had made for him to ward off the fire of dragons, but even if he had been a famous dragon-slayer in his youth he did not succeed this time. His expedition against Northumbria ended in disaster and capture by King Aella, who had him thrown into a pit of snakes.

It is said that Ragnar Lodbrok met his end well, delivering a dire threat to his enemy and a death-song in the form of heroic verse – no mean feat while being bitten to death by snakes. In any case, his dragon-proof trousers failed to save him from snakebites and Ragnar succumbed after making a final prediction of revenge by his sons, whose forces arrived in southern England rather than landing directly on the Northumbrian coast.

Northumbria

Landing in East Anglia allowed the Vikings to make preparations for their expedition against Northumbria. The latter was a powerful kingdom, stretching up the east side of Great Britain from the River Humber to the Forth, and included holdings on the west coast. It was created from the smaller kingdoms of Bernica and Deira in 604 AD. Northumbria embraced Christianity in 627 AD and was an important centre for religion. By the early 700s AD, however, the kingdom was in decline and at the time of the Viking invasion it was greatly diminished.

It is known that the Great Army (sometimes known as the Great Heathen Army) met no real resistance in East Anglia and pushed north in 866 AD. Half of the Viking invasion force marched overland while the remainder sailed into the River Humber. Their progress was accompanied by the usual pillaging, with many holy sites, including Whitby Abbey, sacked. The Northumbrians were suffering from an internal dispute and relatively little resistance was encountered until the Vikings reached York in November of 866 AD.

The invaders spent the winter in York, putting the time to good use by repairing the Roman fortifications there. In March of 867 AD, the Northumbrian army attacked the invaders. After defeating this force, the Vikings were able to capture more towns and installed a puppet king. If the invasion had begun as a raid in force, it had become a campaign of conquest.

Wessex and Mercia

After taking control of Northumbria, the Vikings turned south and came into conflict with the kingdom of Mercia, which had been asked by Northumbria to help resist the invaders. The Vikings captured Nottingham but did not conquer Mercia for a few more years. Instead, they returned to East Anglia in 870 AD. The East Anglian army was defeated and King Edmund killed, placing the region under Viking control.

Strengthened in 871 AD by a force known as the Great Summer Army, the Great Army made war upon both Wessex and Mercia. Despite some victories, including the capture of Reading, the Vikings were unable to defeat their opponents and agreed to withdraw in return

BELOW: **Alfred the Great is sometimes considered to be the great king and defender of the English. His success in warding off the Viking invasion earned him a place in history and legend.**

for a bribe. They turned their attention northwards, sending part of their force to fight the Picts, while the remainder made preparations for renewed conflict in the south.

The Vikings were distracted in 872 AD by a rebellion in Northumbria, and were content for a time to accept bribes (which would eventually become known as Danegeld) to leave Mercia alone. However, in 874 AD the Vikings felt that the time was right and pushed into Mercia, defeating local forces and driving out the king.

By 875 AD, a Viking kingdom centred upon Jorvik (York) was well established. The area under Viking control became known as the *Danelaw*, although the term also had other applications. With their power well established, the Vikings of the Great Army launched a new campaign into Wessex. Their chief opponent was King Alfred of Wessex, the only English monarch ever to earn the title of 'The Great'. Alfred had risen to the throne upon the death of his brother Aethelred in 871 AD and had immediately to deal with Viking incursions. He was probably not surprised by the renewal of hostilities.

The Great Army was at this time led by Guthorm, who had acquired other areas of England over the preceding years and in 876 AD felt he was in a good position to take Wessex. Rather than smash their way through the Wessex defences, the Vikings bypassed them and advanced quickly into the interior. Their strategy was often to grab a town by surprise attack and to hang onto it until bribed to leave. Guthorm's host advanced all the way to the Dorset coast and occupied Wareham.

'OFTEN IS THERE REGRET FOR SAYING TOO MUCH, AND SELDOM REGRET FOR SAYING TOO LITTLE.'

Despite receiving reinforcements by sea, Guthorm became besieged in Wareham and was forced to negotiate a peace treaty, which he immediately broke and attempted to escape. Part of his army reached Exeter while other forces attempted to flee by sea and were scattered by storms. Guthorm negotiated another treaty, accepting a large bribe to retreat out of Wessex.

The Vikings wintered around Gloucester but returned to Wessex early in 878 AD with a surprise attack, almost catching

Alfred in his winter quarters. His resistance thereafter took the form of a guerrilla campaign until he was able to raise a new army capable of challenging the invaders. They met at the battle of Ethandun, where the Vikings were decisively defeated. They took refuge in Chippenham but were starved into submission and forced to swear yet another peace treaty.

This treaty was much the same as the others thus far between the Great Army and Wessex. It involved the same oaths and hostage exchanges as the previous arrangements, plus the requirement that Guthorm be baptized into the Christian faith. However, this time the circumstances were different. The Vikings had been soundly beaten rather than fought to a standstill, and they had political troubles of their own. The Great Army was breaking up under the stress of disagreements between various Viking leaders, and it was doubtful whether Guthorm could maintain the offensive. That being the case he decided to honour this new treaty and withdrew from Wessex. He ruled as king in East Anglia thereafter.

ABOVE: According to legend, King Alfred obtained strategic intelligence by disguising himself as a minstrel and performing for Viking king Guthorm. Learning that the Viking force was short of food, Alfred was able to formulate a winning strategy.

End of an Era

Viking raids against England continued of course, and indeed the new Viking overlords within the Danelaw also suffered the depredations of their kin from the homelands. However, the era of the greatest Viking raids was coming to an end by 900 AD. Various European rulers, including Alfred the Great, took measures to defend against the raiders. Bridges were fortified to impede penetration of the rivers, and some rulers began to build fleets to defend the coasts.

OPPOSITE: **By the early 900s, the Vikings had conquered large areas of England and were part of the political landscape there rather than an external force. Raids were still ongoing, both for plunder and as part of a larger campaign of conquest.**

Alfred the Great ordered the construction of a new fleet in 896 AD. The vessels constructed were large and powerful compared to the Viking longships, but were probably not as seaworthy. However, they did not need to be as their role was coastal defence, not long-distance voyages, and the emphasis on fighting power over seaworthiness gave them an advantage when they met Viking ships. These were not the first warships operated by an English kingdom, but they did represent a new confidence and determination to meet the raiders at sea and defeat them.

Alfred also reorganized the military forces of Wessex and their tactics, constructing fortifications to oppose a landing and marching inland to fortify towns. Perhaps most importantly these forts provided early warning of an incursion and could slow the raiders, allowing Alfred time to assemble sufficient forces to beat them back. Although these measures were not sufficient to defeat the Vikings completely, they took the form of what today might be called 'target-hardening', making the traditional fast Viking raid difficult to accomplish. Effectively, Alfred the Great deterred raids by increasing the difficulty-to-gain ratio to an unacceptable level.

A large Viking force did attempt to seize land in southern England in 892 or 893 AD. This was not a raid as such but an attempted land grab – the Vikings brought their families from the continent and were hoping to settle rather than plunder. Despite some early success they were met with a robust response from Wessex and were scattered, failing to establish a firm foothold or new settlements.

Other rulers were less successful than Alfred at dealing with Viking incursions, but the golden age of raiding at will was very much over. Viking attacks continued to inspire fear, but they were likely to be met with force on land or at sea by people who at least now knew what they were dealing with. Many of the coasts previously raided were now the territory of Viking settlers, who might or might not become target for further raids.

Kissing the Foot of the King

In France, King Charles III came up with a novel solution to the problem of Viking raids – he would gift land to Viking settlers in return for them defending his coast. He entered into a deal with

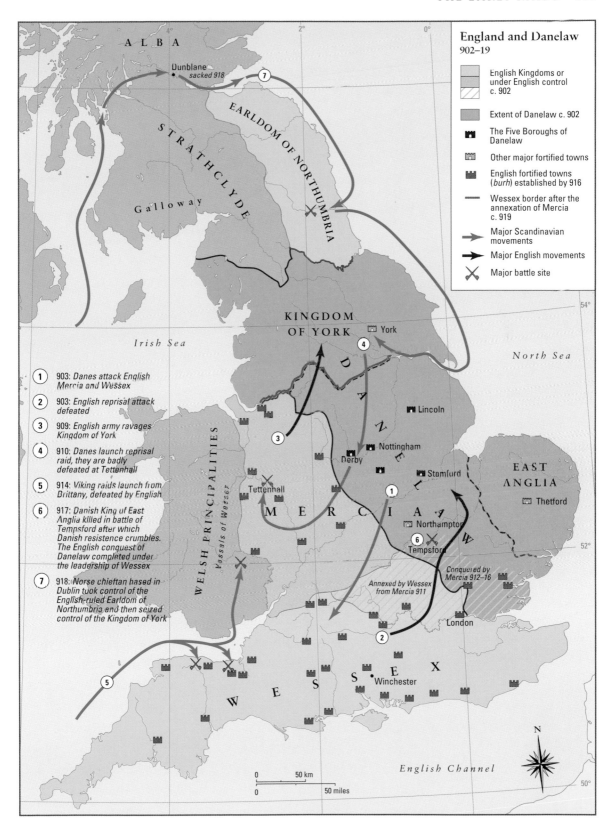

England and Danelaw
902–19

<table>
<tr><td>█</td><td>English Kingdoms or under English control c. 902</td></tr>
<tr><td>▨</td><td>Extent of Danelaw c. 902</td></tr>
<tr><td>🏰</td><td>The Five Boroughs of Danelaw</td></tr>
<tr><td>🏰</td><td>Other major fortified towns</td></tr>
<tr><td>🏰</td><td>English fortified towns (burh) established by 916</td></tr>
<tr><td>—</td><td>Wessex border after the annexation of Mercia c. 919</td></tr>
<tr><td>→</td><td>Major Scandinavian movements</td></tr>
<tr><td>➜</td><td>Major English movements</td></tr>
<tr><td>✕</td><td>Major battle site</td></tr>
</table>

A L B A

Dunblane · *sacked 918*

⑦

EARLDOM OF NORTHUMBRIA

S T R A T H C L Y D E

Galloway

Irish Sea

KINGDOM OF YORK

④ 🏰 York

North Sea

D A N E L A W

🏰 Lincoln

KINGDOM OF YORK

③

Derby 🏰 🏰 Nottingham

① 903: Danes attack English Mercia and Wessex

② 903: English reprisal attack defeated

③ 909: English army ravages Kingdom of York

④ 910: Danes launch reprisal raid, they are badly defeated at Tettenhall

⑤ 914: Viking raids launch from Brittany, defeated by English

⑥ 917: Danish King of East Anglia killed in battle of Tempsford after which Danish resistence crumbles. The English conquest of Danelaw completed under the leadership of Wessex

⑦ 918: Norse chieftan based in Dublin took control of the English-ruled Earldom of Northumbria and then seized control of the Kingdom of York

W E L S H   P R I N C I P A L I T I E S
Vassals of Wessex

🏰 Tettenhall

M E R C I A

① 🏰 Stamford

EAST ANGLIA

🏰 Thetford

🏰 Northampton

⑥ ✕ Tempsford

Conquered by Mercia 912–16

Annexed by Wessex from Mercia 911

② London

W E S S E X

· Winchester

🏰

⑤

English Channel

N

0   50 km

0   50 miles

ABOVE: **Paris was not a capital city when it was besieged by the Vikings in 885 AD, but it did have significant defences. The Vikings were by this time capable of conducting complex large-scale operations to reduce a city's defences. They were no longer simply opportunistic sea-raiders.**

the Viking leader Rollo, whose origin is disputed by historians. Some believe that Rollo was the son of a west-Norwegian nobleman; others suggest he was an exiled Dane. Whichever was the case, he seems to have risen to prominence as a leader among the Viking force that besieged Paris in 885 AD. His first deal with Charles, King of the West Franks, was to accept tribute in return for raiding against Charles' enemies elsewhere. During his second attack on Paris he was offered the region of Normandy as his territory if he would swear allegiance to Charles and accept baptism. His duties as ruler of Normandy (historians disagree as to whether his title was Count or Duke) included the defence of the coast against future raiders.

According to popular history, Rollo displayed some of the Vikings' traditional attributes when he was asked to pledge allegiance to Charles III – pride and a rather robust sense of humour. The custom of the time was for the vassal to kiss the ruler's foot, which Rollo considered humiliating. The deal almost fell through at this point, but it was eventually agreed that one of Rollo's warriors would perform the gesture in his place.

The warrior was supposed to bend down and kiss Charles' foot, but for whatever reason he decided instead to seize the king of France's foot and lift it to his lips. He must have known what would ensue, and the fact that he was willing to make an act that could be seen as insulting and might trigger conflict suggests either an excess of courage or a complete lack of regard for the consequences. Either way, King Charles III was tipped over backwards and fell to the ground, to the great amusement of Rollo and his Vikings.

However, the shoe was kissed and the deal was made. Charles III got his border defenders and Rollo got his land. If the occasion was not quite as solemn as some had hoped then that was perhaps the price of doing business with Vikings.

Rollo's pledge of allegiance to Charles III marks a change in the nature of Viking existence. The raids did not stop, of course, but the situation had become a lot more complex. No longer simply sea-raiders out of Scandinavia, the Vikings now came as settlers and sometimes conquerors. They had become players on the chessboard of European politics rather than simply snatching the occasional random piece off it.

LEFT: **Paying the Vikings not to raid was a dangerous strategy, but it worked to the advantage of King Charles. He was able to send the raiders against his rivals, weakening them while avoiding having his own territory ravaged.**

6

VIKING WEAPONS AND COMBAT

The Vikings were warriors, not soldiers as such. Few of them were professionals in the field of arms, but most men owned weapons and were shown how to use them by their friends and relatives as they grew up. This suggests that the majority of Vikings in a battle will have used fairly unsophisticated techniques.

Those who survived a battle would pass on their observations about what had worked and what had not, and an accepted body of technique would have existed. To these basic moves would be added more tricky or subtle techniques developed by experienced fighters and taught to their friends. Those who fought a lot or could afford the time to train properly with their weapons would outclass men who simply owned an axe or sword and swung it with determination but little skill.

There is little first-hand information on how the Vikings fought, but it is possible to reconstruct their fighting style from various sources. The sagas mention a range of clever stratagems

OPPOSITE: **Later depictions of Vikings tend to contain numerous anachronisms. Breastplates, chainmail trews and winged helmets come from the imagination of the artist rather than historical accuracy.**

RIGHT: Much can be
learned from skeletal
remains about the
Vikings' weaponry
and fighting systems.
The location of wounds
and the impressions
left on bones can help
indicate the sort of
blows that were struck,
and thus how Viking
warriors fought.

used in combat and also some quite incredible moves. Most of
these are physically possible, so it is conceivable that things may
have occurred as described. In some cases these may even have
been standard tactics that warriors trained to perform.

The remains of people killed in battle can give an idea of the
location and nature of their wounds and, when combined with
practical experiments with similar weapons, this creates a picture
of the sort of blows that were struck. It is not possible to be
absolutely certain as to exactly how these blows were executed,
but in all likelihood the simplest explanation is the correct one.
A man fighting for his life will not do something complicated
when there is a quicker, easier and more sure way to accomplish
the same task.

On Land and at Sea

Combat on a larger scale was highly individualistic, with a
warband fighting as a group of armed men rather than a neatly
arranged formation of soldiers. This does not, however, mean
that the Vikings could not cooperate or use formations. Men
who knew one another well and who had perhaps fought
together before could support one another and predict the others'
responses to any given situation, protecting a friend who needed
time to recover from a dropped weapon or minor wound, or
assisting someone who was outnumbered or outmatched.

The Vikings did use one well-ordered battle formation known as the *Svinfylking*, or 'Swine Array'. This was a wedge formation and, predictably perhaps, was primarily used for offensive movements. It is probable that the outermost men, at the front of the wedge, were the best armed and armoured, but a man wishing to be seen as courageous might demand a place in the front line despite a lack of armour.

The Swine Array was a potent weapon in breaking through a shield wall, one of the other common battle formations of the day. A shield wall, formed by warriors locking their overlapping shields together, could be highly successful at fending off attacks by many individual warriors, but could be broken by the momentum of an aggressive wedge. Once the wall was broken, combat would probably break up into individual and small-group melees in which the Viking fighting style was highly effective.

A simple formation like a wedge or wall is relatively easy to form, even for untrained warriors, but can be unwieldy if movement is required. Complex battlefield evolutions and changes of formation require a level of training that can only be imposed on troops who are at least semi-professional. Thus

BELOW: A shield wall was the standard defensive formation of the era, normally composed of a single line of shields. Doubling up like this limited the ability of warriors to fight but offered improved protection against arrows.

the Vikings and their enemies could form a wedge or wall when needed, but anything more complex was likely to fail.

This style of fighting perfectly suited the Vikings and was well tailored to their environment. Most combat was between small bands engaged in feuding and raiding, and until the rise of the larger Viking kingdoms, not even kings fielded major armies. In an environment where a major battle might involve a few hundred warriors there was no need and little opportunity for large-scale formations.

Combat at sea was not all that different from fighting on land. Ships did not mount projectile weapons or rams. Combat was a matter of approaching another ship and launching arrows, followed by a close approach and hand-to-hand combat. It was common for a warrior to stand in the prow of the ship and engage his opposite number, with other men stepping up when a champion was killed or injured. In other cases a desperate melee took place in the poor footing of a small and cluttered ship, with aggression and a certain amount of luck being every bit as important as skill at arms.

BELOW: In order to transfer personnel from one vessel to another, or to fight, ships had to be brought close together. This required skilled seamanship, as an error could entangle or break some of the oars.

Shiphandling skills were important to this sort of fighting when moving the vessel into a favourable attack position, and skilled archery could decide a battle before boarding took place. There was no place for anything but the most rudimentary mutual assistance either between ships or the fighters aboard one. Battle on land or at sea was a matter of every man doing his utmost and relying on his comrades to do the same.

The Vikings fought on foot, although they were happy to use horses for transport, and their arms and equipment were well suited to their very personal style of combat. The belief that their fate was preordained meant that Vikings used very aggressive tactics. There were two possible outcomes from a fight: either the warrior would be killed or he would not. It had already been decided which was to occur, and there was nothing the warrior could do about it. So why not set about him and do as much damage as possible? He could not determine whether he lived through the battle or died, but he had a choice about the amount of word-fame he won.

Shields

Vikings did defend of course, and indeed defence was integral to a skilled warrior's fighting style, but their ultimate goal was the destruction of the enemy rather than personal survival. Ironically, a warrior who is fighting to win is often more likely to survive a battle than one who is merely trying to stay alive, as the former will take his opponents out of the fight quickly, or at least force them onto the defensive where they are less likely to land a telling blow.

Most warriors were protected by a shield, which was typically round and constructed either of wooden boards or planks. Some shields were reinforced with iron bands, and there was an iron boss at the centre. Shield sizes varied somewhat, as a good shield was matched to the wielder's arm length. It was not a passive defence, like a mobile wall to hide behind, but an integral part of the Viking warrior's fighting style. It was used in a mobile and even aggressive manner, to attack as well as defend, and for some

ABOVE: The shield was as much a weapon as a defensive tool. It could be used to strike or to block an opponent, and could be pressed against his weapon arm to prevent him from striking at all. It was better used to deflect or intercept blows than to block them square on.

ABOVE: **A warrior's shield covered and protected much of his body, and just as importantly it prevented an opponent seeing much of him. The sword could be concealed behind the shield, creating doubt about where the warrior intended to strike.**

actions that were somewhere in between. To be useful in this manner a shield had to be light enough to wield effectively yet large enough to provide adequate cover.

The most basic defence with a shield was to hold it in front of you and hope blows landed on it. This was the only real defence against arrows, and was reasonably effective. Even just holding a shield up in this manner was tiring, and not entirely effective. Someone armed with an axe or perhaps a sword could attack a shield held in this manner and quickly reduce it to uselessness, opening up the user to further blows.

To avoid the quick destruction of the shield, a skilled warrior used it in a much more active manner. One counter to an overhead blow was to move in with the shield presented horizontally and the edge driving forward at the attacker's face. Ideally, the attacker's sword arm, not his weapon, would contact the shield. This avoided damage to the shield while stopping the blow, and possibly allowed a jabbing strike to the face with the rim. It also concealed the defender's weapon arm.

Protected overhead by his shield, the defender was well positioned to thrust with a sword at the opponent's body. Even if he guessed where the blow was coming from, the attacker's attempt to intercept the strike with his own shield would be hampered by the shield in his face. Alternatively, the defender could cut with sword or axe at the attacker's leg. Wounds of this sort, on the outside of the leg, are fairly common on the skeletons of Viking warriors that have been studied.

A good sword or axe blow would bite into a shield and might split it, although Viking shields were surprisingly resistant to being hacked apart. One defensive tactic was to allow the opponent's sword to drive into the rim of the shield, hoping that it would be trapped there. The weapon could then be twisted out of the opponent's hand or bent into uselessness.

As well as being a physical barrier a shield also blocked sight. Presented well forward, it made it difficult for the opponent to see much of his target, which concealed the shield user's intentions and limited his opponent's options. A skilled shield user could take advantage of this to make his opponent's attacks predictable. This in turn made a decisive counter possible, ending the fight. Conversely, he could prolong the fight to wear out or humiliate his opponent.

'BETTER A BRIEF SPELL OF HONOUR THAN A LONG RULE OF SHAME.'

Shield Bind

One highly effective shield technique was the 'shield bind', whereby the movement of the opponent's weapon arm was impaired by pushing the shield against it. With the opponent's shield pressed hard against the outside of his upper arm, a warrior could not swing his sword and could be controlled quite effectively. A shield bind could be applied after successfully blocking a cut with the shield, or by advancing against the opponent and pushing his weapon arm aside. It was a useful way to set up a sword thrust to the body, as the shield concealed the user's weapon and thus his intentions.

A shield could be used to strike a powerful blow with the central heavy iron boss or the rim, or to batter an opponent backwards. Holding his shield close to his body and concealing as much of himself behind it as possible, the warrior charged into his opponent. The boss might cause injury, and the opponent might be knocked backwards off balance or even caused to fall, while the attacker was well protected against a potential counter-blow.

The tactic of driving an opponent back with the shield and then hitting him with a weapon while he was staggering or off balance was a fairly basic one, requiring little more than determination and a reasonable amount of body mass, so it was probably a staple move used by many Viking warriors. The shield was extremely useful in combat, and even someone who did not really know how to use one would benefit from it. Not surprisingly, there were several techniques for getting an opponent's shield out of the way. However, at times he might voluntarily give up its use.

There are accounts in the sagas of warriors who slung their shields on their backs in order to make better use of a weapon in both hands, and at times shields were thrown over downed friends to protect them from further harm. Casting away the shield was a powerful symbolic gesture as well, essentially proclaiming an intention to focus 100 per cent on offence, which could be intimidating to enemies.

Cloaks

Not all Viking warriors possessed armour of any sort, so the shield was extremely important and its loss would be keenly felt. In an emergency a cloak or other item of clothing could be used for defence purposes. One method that had been postulated would be to wrap the cloak around the arm and use it to parry with, but this is questionable. A sharp weapon might well cut through to cause grave injury, and the author's experiment with a backsword – a lighter weapon than the Viking sword or axe – suggests that the parrying arm will not remain useable for long, even if it is not cut.

It is more likely that a cloak would be held or partially wrapped around the arm and the dangling folds used to entangle a weapon. This could be done quite passively, just by holding the arm up and hoping the cut passed through the folds, or by sweeping the cloak so that it entangled the weapon and dragged it aside. This method offers a much better defence against a spear or sword thrust than hanging a curtain in the way and hoping for the best.

Rather than being held, a cloak could be thrown over an opponent's weapon, disabling it briefly until he disentangled himself. It could also be thrown over his head to blind him or simply thrown in his general direction as a distraction. There are numerous examples in the sagas of fights being stopped (usually by women) by throwing clothing onto the combatants' weapons. Any fairly heavy piece of cloth would suffice, which given the cold conditions of the Viking homelands meant any item of outdoor clothing was a potential fight-stopper.

For those who could afford it, the additional protection
of armour made them formidable opponents. Armour was
sometimes improvised; the sagas speak of warriors placing flat
stones within their clothing, or using hide or horn to create
effective, if clumsy, armour. A number of saga-heroes have lucky
escapes when a blow hits the only thing they are carrying that
could have stopped it, such as a wineskin on the back under
a cloak when the wearer was ambushed. Mostly, such events
are in the interest of a good story or can be attributed to the
preordained fate awaiting these heroes – it was not their time, so
an otherwise perfect blow somehow failed to cause injury.

ABOVE: The mail-shirt
was an expensive item
but offered excellent
protection to those who
could afford one. Mail
is flexible and, although
heavy, it does not impair
movement in the way
that solid plates can.

Chainmail

Armour was a much more sure defence. The best available was
mail, which offered good protection but was expensive and
available only to very rich warriors. Mail protection is usually
referred to in the sagas as *Brynja*, i.e. a mail-shirt. It typically took
a similar form to the warrior's over-tunic, although with shorter
sleeves that reached just past the elbow or mid-forearm. Sleeves
were loose, allowing the arms to move freely. In essence, a mail-
shirt was a large tube that covered the body and had holes for the
arms, with two smaller and shorter tubes as sleeves. It was put
on over the head and belted at the waist. If its overall shape was
simple, however, its construction was rather more complex.

Mail was composed of small metal rings, which became finer later in the Viking Age. Normally each ring passed through four others, although a more complex 'double layered' mail is referred to in some sagas. In this case the rings are doubled up, with each pair passing through four other pairs. Although it would provide better protection, double-layer mail would be heavier, which would tire the wearer and possibly making him more vulnerable in a long fight. It would also take more than twice as long to make, and require far more materials. There are mentions of double-layered mail in some sagas, but it is rare even by the standards of conventional armour, which was by no means prevalent.

BELOW: A padded jerkin or thick leather tunic offered some protection from blows, and may have been worn under mail by some warriors. Mail backed by padding is an excellent form of armour but its existence in the Viking Age is hard to prove.

Producing a mail-shirt was a huge undertaking in terms of both time and materials. A large amount of iron was needed to make the rings, and this did not come cheap. Nor did the armour-maker's time. Viking mail consisted of alternating solid rings and 'open' rings, which were secured with rivets after being put in place. Butted rings, where the ends were simply pushed together, were quicker and therefore cheaper to work with, but were far more vulnerable to damage.

Forming the rings into mail was an intricate and time-consuming process, and before it could even begin the rings themselves had to be made. Solid rings could be formed from a sheet of metal beaten to the required thickness, while open rings were formed from wire, which was made by drawing iron through a series of ever-smaller holes, eventually creating a thick wire that could then be cut to the desired length. Finer mail, made in the later years of the Viking Age, was lighter but took even longer to produce as the wire had to be drawn more times.

Additional Protection

It is possible that some mail-shirts had a backing material, perhaps leather or thick padded cloth, but most were simply a shirt of mail. This offered excellent protection against a glancing cut or a weak thrust, as it prevented the sharp or pointed weapon from penetrating, and it would spread out the impact of an axe blade or sword edge, hopefully making such a blow survivable. A heavy blow could still cause serious injury even if the mail was not broken, so some sort of additional protection was desirable.

It is likely that a padded jerkin or something similar was worn under mail by at least some warriors, although evidence of this is hard to come by. A skeleton has been found with the marks of mail rings on his leg bones, suggesting that a mighty blow drove the mail links right through his skin and muscle. Some form of padding might have prevented this, and that would have been obvious to the warriors of the time. Thus, although little archaeological evidence exists, it is quite likely that the warriors of the Viking Age knew how to protect themselves adequately.

> 'ILL IT IS TO ABANDON HONOR AND INTEGRITY IN EXCHANGE FOR INJUSTICE AND GREED.'

For those who could not afford a proper mail-shirt, lesser or no protection had to suffice. A thick leather or hide jerkin offered a measure of defence against less than perfect blows. It might even prevent an axe or sword from cutting and absorb some of the impact, but a clean hit or a thrust from a spear or sword would punch right through this sort of armour.

Helmets and Head Protection

Adding a small amount of mail at critical spots increased the effectiveness of this lighter armour. Many blows came from overhead, so obtaining some head protection was perhaps the most effective measure short of buying an entire mail-shirt. Some helmets had mail attached to them, covering the neck and shoulders where many high blows landed. A warrior with a good helmet was better protected than one whose head was undefended, and this was enormously cheaper than mail.

Some Viking helmets had mail attached, but all of them lacked horns. The 'horned helmet' popularly associated with Viking warriors is simply a myth. Apart from anything else, it would have been a serious impediment, even when not in combat. Horns would catch on ropes aboard ship or on the helmets of other

BELOW: **With a shield in front and the head and shoulders protected by a good helmet with a hood of mail attached, a Viking warrior was well protected even if he could not afford a mail-shirt.**

RIGHT: Some Viking helmets had protection for the upper face. A nasal bar added little weight and improved protection considerably. Eye protection may not have added much to the helmet's effectiveness, and may have been more for intimidation.

Vikings, leading to entanglements and perhaps brawls long before the enemy were sighted. They would also unbalance the helmet and make it more likely to fall off.

In battle, blows that would otherwise miss would strike these protruding horns, at best yanking the wearer's head around in a painful manner or pulling his helmet off. They might even redirect onto the helmet a blow that would otherwise have gone past. All of this would have increased the vulnerability of the wearer – something the helmet is supposed to reduce. The pragmatic Viking warrior would probably have found the idea of a horned helmet quite hilarious.

Most Viking helmets were formed from several metal pieces fixed together rather than being a single piece hammered into shape. The latter is stronger but much more difficult to produce, which might explain the Viking preference for constructed helmets. The usual form was a circular iron band as the base, with a pair of bands crossing over and riveted to the main circlet. Leather could be fixed to these to offer moderate protection but iron plates were better. This created a solid dome of metal to protect the head.

Some helmets included eye protection in the form of a mask with eyeholes, forming what was effectively a pair of metal goggles with no lenses. Protection of this sort was effective against, say, a sword cut across the face, but a thrust with the point of a sword or spear could be caught by the eyeholes. This was not necessarily much worse than it would otherwise have been; a thrust that was redirected into the eye was probably going to hit the helmet's wearer in the face regardless.

Whatever the relative merits of the eye protection, it may have existed purely to intimidate opponents. Most helmets lacked this sort of protection, although a nasal bar was common. This was a vertical projection downwards in front of the face. Again, it was effective against a cut or other blow across the face and much less so against a thrust.

The helmet did not simply sit on the wearer's head. If it did, then it might offer some protection against a glancing blow but a solid contact with sword or axe would be little different in effect to striking directly on the skull. The helmet dome was kept clear of the head by padding inside. Thus the helmet protected its wearer by preventing a sharp edge from cutting his head and by deflecting some of the impact of the blow. The padding cushioned this further, making a head blow less likely to debilitate the user.

The helmet was only useful if it stayed on, of course. It is likely that most Viking helmets had some form of chinstrap, although little archaeological evidence has been found. Jamming a helmet on tight, like a hat on a windy day, would work only up to a point – the first horizontal blow would knock it off. Battlefields would soon become littered with dislodged helmets, and survivors of the conflict would surely begin searching for a means to prevent losing

BELOW: **Horned helmets might have had some ceremonial role, but they had no place in battle. Horns make a helmet less effective and can cost the wearer his life, so it is rather unlikely that Viking warriors would favour them.**

their head protection. Apart from anything else, a well-made helmet was a costly item and its loss could wipe out all the profit a warrior made from an expedition.

Heavy Going

A warrior's personal protection, i.e. his helmet and mail, were a form of life insurance, but they were also heavy. The weight of this kind of armour is more noticeable when it is picked up and carried rather than when it is worn. The weight of a mail-shirt is fairly well distributed and is carried by the shoulders and hips, where it is secured with a belt. A good mail-shirt allowed freedom of movement, and the user was likely to find it tiring to wear rather than heavy.

Armour did not make any given movement more difficult, but did make it more tiring by forcing the user to expend more energy each time he took a step or swung a sword. Fatigue could be a killer; a tired fighter would not react quickly to an opening and would miss chances to end a fight. Conversely he would be easier to hit. Armour did not offer total protection, but while a fighter was moving about a lot it was hard to land the sort of clean blow that would defeat his armour. As he tired and slowed, it became easier to batter him to death with heavy blows even if his armour held out.

RIGHT: A sword and axe head found in a Viking burial. It was common for a man to be buried with his weapons and the tools of his trade. Finding a sword or axe in a grave does not necessarily mean that a man was a professional warrior of course; most Viking men owned weapons.

Some parts of the body were unprotected by a mail-shirt and helmet, including the lower legs and arms as well as the face in many cases. Thus armour was by no means a guarantee of safety on the battlefield, and was sometimes left behind even by those who could afford it. Given the choice between grabbing his shield and donning a mail-shirt, the typical Viking would opt for the shield. His weapons took precedence over both.

Swords

The most famous weapon associated with the Vikings is also one of the rarest – swords were difficult to make and consumed more good-quality iron than spearheads or axe blades. Thus they were extremely expensive and were often handed down as heirlooms. The decision whether to place a man's sword on his funeral pyre or hand it on to his eldest son must have been a difficult one.

The typical Viking sword is shorter than most modern people would imagine, and a lot less heavy. Video games and certain movies tend to depict people waving around something that resembles a surf board with a handle, but the reality is that a huge sword would be impossible to control and thus a liability in combat. In order to take effect, a cut must be delivered at the right time and with good body mechanics that allow the edge to bite and the mass of the sword to push it into the target. The cut can then be dragged or pushed to widen or deepen it. Whether the cut lands or not, it is necessary to recover the weapon, i.e. return it to a position where it can be used to deliver more blows.

A weapon that is too heavy is difficult to get moving at the right time and in the right direction, and will drag the user off balance as he tries to recover it. Such a sword may deliver a massive blow, but this is little use if it exposes the wielder to a strike by other enemies or someone whose shield and/or armour have protected him.

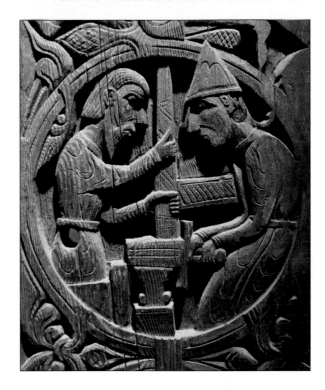

ABOVE: This carving shows Regin the Smith reforging Sigurd's broken sword. Some repairs were very crude, but a skilled craftsman could return a blade to combat effectiveness much more cheaply than forging a new weapon.

RIGHT: Normally concealed by the handgrip, the tang is a critically important part of a sword blade. If it is weak it may snap, causing the blade to part company with the rest of the weapon. A bent tang will also render the weapon impossible to wield effectively.

BELOW: The pommel could be used to hook a shield or strike with, but its main function was as a counterweight for the blade. An excessively blade-heavy weapon is hard to control, which can make the user very vulnerable.

The Viking sword was a simple design intended to be used in one hand, usually in conjunction with a shield. The blade was designed primarily for vigorous cutting strokes with both edges, although the 'long edge' – the edge facing away from the user when the sword was held vertically in the hand – was mostly used. This was later referred to as the 'true edge'. The sword could also thrust, although the somewhat rounded tip of most blades required a fair amount of force to push through flesh. Rather crude single-edged swords did exist, but they were not common.

The weapon overall was typically about 100cm (39in) long, including the handgrip and a pommel that served as a counterweight for the blade. These were not 'fencing' swords, intended for both attack and defence, and had little hand protection, although some designs had a crosspiece. This prevented an opponent's blade sliding up the sword into the user's hand. It is unlikely that the crosspiece was used to trap an opponent's blade as in later, e.g. medieval, styles of swordsmanship, as the Vikings did not fight in that manner. The sword was primarily for attacking and the shield for defence.

The sword was created in separate parts, of which the blade was the most important. In order to create a blade with the necessary combination of hardness and flexibility, a complex process called pattern-welding was used. By braiding iron strips with slightly different composition, the swordsmith created a bar that was then heated, hammered flat and shaped into a sword blade. Pattern welding became less common in later periods as steel-making processes improved, although some swords were still made this way for decorative reasons. A pattern-welded sword blade was strong enough to remain useful in combat where a softer iron blade would simply bend, and flexible enough to survive impacts. It would take a good edge but would lose it fairly quickly, so often the edges of the sword were formed from hard steel strips that would resist blunting for longer.

A sword that became blunt was still useful as a metal club, but would require a lot of effort to cause a disabling wound to an opponent. More seriously, swords would bend or even snap in combat, making them useless. Even a weapon that survived would need maintenance after a hard fight, and repairs were undertaken several times in the lives of many swords. Examples have been found that have clearly been broken and reforged, which required considerably less effort than creating a new blade out of raw iron.

At the rear of the blade was a projection called the tang, which fitted into a hilt that was made separately. A damaged hilt could be replaced, as could a bent or broken blade. It is possible that during a long career a sword might have both, like the proverbial everlasting broom that has had seven new heads and three new shafts. A sword, unlike a broom, had an identity and was often given a name, so presumably its spirit lived on in the weapon as a whole, despite the replacement of constituent parts.

Scabbards

A sword was carried in a scabbard to protect it and to prevent accidental injury to those nearby; there are numerous references in the sagas to swords without associated scabbards causing trouble for their users. However, it was also a fairly common practice to enter combat with the sword already drawn and hanging from a thong around the warrior's hand. He could fight with a spear in this manner, dropping it when it broke or became stuck in a target, and instantly have his sword to hand.

Sword scabbards also caused problems from time to time; more than one saga-hero finds his weapon stuck in its scabbard when

BELOW: **This modern replica shows the deceptively simple form of the Viking sword. Although unsophisticated it was a robust and effective weapon that could give decades of service if properly maintained.**

he needs it. It is not clear whether these setbacks are part of a good story, giving the hero additional problems to overcome, or if this was a common occurrence. Either way, a warrior struggling to free his weapon was in serious danger.

'IT CAN BE EXPECTED THAT A MAN WHO HAS A LOT ON HIS MIND WILL NOT ALWAYS BE CAREFUL ENOUGH.'

The scabbard was made from wood, often lined with wool, and had a metal chape at the tip to prevent the sword from poking through the end. Some scabbards were reinforced with metal at the throat, helping them to keep their shape. Perhaps this was a reason for a weapon to become stuck – a deformed throat of the scabbard would jam the weapon within or make it difficult to put away after a fight.

A scabbarded sword was normally carried on the belt, especially in the later Viking Era. Earlier it was common to attach the scabbard to a shoulder belt so that it hung at the waist, or sometimes to hang it on the back. Although there are references in the sagas to warriors carrying their swords on their back and drawing them over the shoulder, these would be ordinary swords and not long-two-handed swords that have to be carried in this fashion. The Vikings did not favour such long weapons, perhaps because they lacked the metallurgy to produce one that would not break. A two-handed grip was sometimes used to add power to a swing, but a sword constructed specifically for two-handed use was not a Viking weapon.

BELOW: **The knife was for working rather than fighting, and few Vikings would be without one. It could be used to finish off an opponent or as a weapon of desperation, but it was primarily viewed as a tool.**

The Sax

A sword is, to some extent, an overgrown knife and is made in a similar way. However, it is much quicker, simpler and cheaper to produce a good knife, and, being shorter, knives are not subject to the same stresses as a sword blade. Even a knife made out of fairly inferior iron would last a long time. The sagas include several instances of warriors having to stamp on their swords to straighten them, but a knife would probably remain useable right up until the blade broke.

A knife was an indispensable tool for eating, work and occasional bloody violence. In a fight it was not much of a weapon, but a small blade was certainly better than nothing. Somewhere between the knife and a true sword was a weapon known as the sax. This was a simple short sword-type weapon with a single cutting edge and no hand protection. It was carried horizontally in a sheath that hung from the belt, with the weapon's edge upwards.

The sax was sometimes obtained as a cheaper alternative to a sword, and was often also carried by those who could afford a proper sword. It served as a backup weapon if the spear, axe or sword were dropped, and could be used with a shield in much the same manner as the sword. It could also be handled much like a knife and used when grappling with an opponent. Some Viking warriors and saga heroes are said to have preferred to fight at close quarters with the sax than to use a sword or larger weapon. Others drew their sax at a critical moment to finish off an opponent or to escape from a bad situation.

Axes

The standard Viking hand weapon was the axe, which was much more common than the sword. Axes do not require complex metalwork or high-quality steel, as the blade is not subject to the same stresses as a sword. They are thus much cheaper and also, in many cases, more cost efficient. A sword has only one purpose – to fight other people – but an axe obtained for woodcutting and similar work will serve as a reasonable weapon if needed.

Axes produced for war differed somewhat from working tools. The head was often lighter and thinner, as people are less resilient than trees. The head design was generally similar, although combat axes were often 'bearded' with an elongated lower face. This was useful in hooking an opponent's shield and added mass to the head to increase impact.

An axe is a chopping rather than slicing weapon. Its blade increases the effect of a strike by concentrating force, but the weapon is designed to punch deep into flesh rather than slicing

ABOVE: **The sax was somewhere between a knife and a sword, and was useful as a close-quarters weapon. Easier to make and using a smaller quantity of metal, the sax was more affordable than a sword but could be used in a similar manner.**

ABOVE: These replica axes have only a slight 'beard' on the head. Some designs have a very pronounced elongation of the lower cutting face. The angulation of the leftmost axe's head is deliberate, aligning the cutting edge with the arc of a swing.

it open. Effectiveness depends greatly upon impact, and the design of an axe is important if impact is to be maximized. The haft must be of an appropriate length to match the user's arm and thus create a good arc of swing, and the head must concentrate mass behind the blade without making the weapon unwieldy.

Viking axes were thus anything but crude. While less prestigious than swords they were highly effective and were often very well made. Heads were of a socket type, where the head has a hole through which the haft passes. More primitive axes, whose heads are tied on with thongs, were far less effective in action, especially against opponents wearing armour. Even a well-made axe could come apart in combat, however. There are instances in the sagas of axe-heads parting company with the haft, usually to the immediate detriment of the wielder.

The typical Viking axe was wielded in one hand, usually in conjunction with a shield, and had a single cutting blade. The gigantic two-bladed axes often depicted in fantasy games or movies are exactly that – fantasy. The Viking axe was a simple but entirely effective weapon, probably carried without a sheath. It is not hard to stick an axe through a belt, and reasonably safe to carry it this way. One hanging on a thong from the belt would be a rather different proposition, since it would swing about and injure the owner around the knees even if it were not sharp enough to cut him.

Axes could also be carried in other ways. Some saga-heroes and, therefore, presumably some Viking warriors carried an axe in their shield-hand as a backup weapon, transferring it to the weapon hand when the main weapon was lost or hurled at an opponent. They were also fairly concealable, being shorter than most swords, and could be hidden under a cloak or in a bundle of apparently innocuous objects until the wielder was ready to strike.

Long-hafted axes were also used, sometimes as tools and sometimes as weapons. The longer haft required the use of both hands, so the shield had to be cast away or hung on the back. This made the warrior vulnerable, particularly to arrows and

LEFT: Although not as prestigious as a sword, axes were still possessions to be prized. This axe head is beautifully decorated, but that does not preclude it being a working weapon as opposed to a ceremonial or decorative item.

thrown spears, but this was offset by the greater reach and power of his blows. The long-handled axe became a signature weapon of the Varangian Guard in Byzantine service and was adopted by various Viking-influenced cultures, including the English.

An axe, used in one or both hands, was in many ways more capable of penetrating armour than a sword. The combination of leverage, concentration of mass and a sharp blade made an axe more likely to cut through a helmet or bash the wearer senseless, and there are numerous examples of this in the sagas. Less common are descriptions of axes being thrown, although it happens occasionally. When it does, it seems to be an expedient

BELOW: This rather dramatic depiction of Leif Eriksson landing in the New World shows him armed with a long-hafted axe as his primary weapon, with a sword as a backup. He also has a dagger hung vertically from his belt, which may be an anachronism.

BELOW: **This spear point is bronze rather than iron. Bronze deforms more easily than iron and is thus unsuitable for long-bladed weapons, but a spearpoint is not subject to the same stresses as a long blade so will survive longer.**

rather than a planned tactic, suggesting that axes were not normally carried as throwing weapons.

Spears

The spear was another common Viking weapon, not least because it was cheap and relatively easy to make. A spear needs a good shaft, but wood is easier to obtain than metal. The point requires only a small amount of metal and is not complicated to create. Most Viking spear points were simple in design, being leaf-shaped and not particularly long. However, a range of other spear-type weapons were also used.

The names of some weapons have been translated from the sagas as 'halberds' and other weapon types that did not exist in the era. This is understandable, as the translators were comparing the descriptions to weapons they were familiar with, but it can be confusing. Some spear-armed heroes are described as cutting with their weapons, which is a function that the standard spear-point is not well suited to.

While it is possible to cut with the edge of a leaf-shaped spear point, and the edges may well have been sharpened for the purpose, it is more likely that these heroes fought with a different kind of spear. Some warriors may have used broad-headed spears, not unlike the English bill or similar weapons. These would still deliver an effective thrust, but could also make cuts at a distance beyond the reach of a sword or axe. These were known as 'hewing spears' and gave the wielder more options.

Viking spears were not immensely long, with shafts being typically not much over 2m (6.5ft) in length. This created a weapon that had a good reach but was still fairly easy to wield; many spearmen used their weapon in one hand, with a shield, which is difficult when using a very long weapon. A long spear tends to flex under its own weight, causing the tip to wobble about in a manner that makes it hard to aim and is also very tiring on the arm.

Spears were sometimes thrown, and some warriors used a thong to get more power and range from their spear-casts. This was a fairly specialist skill, however, and had the disadvantage that a warrior's supply of spears tended to be fairly limited. Once he had thrown away his weapon, he was down to his sword, axe or sax, unless of course an enemy decided to return it to him by throwing it back.

Bows and Arrows

The spear-cast was a traditional opening move in battle, reflecting Odin's first great spear-throw in battle with the Vanir. Whether or not a good cast doomed the enemy to defeat, taking out a few of their men before closing to use hand weapons was a good option. However, the primary standoff weapon for Vikings was the bow, not the spear.

The Vikings did not make use of massed bodies of archers in the same manner as some later armies, but archery was still a useful tactic. Men used their bows for hunting and would sometimes bring them to a battle or skirmish. They would shoot at the enemy until the two groups closed and then fight with hand weapons; there were no specialist archers in a Viking force.

Bows were very useful in sea combat, extending the reach of warriors aboard a ship. Although the decisive phase of a sea battle involved hand-to-hand fighting in a boarding action, an enemy vessel could be softened up with archery before boarding, and a ship that was evading its enemy or was otherwise difficult to get at – for example in tricky river-mouth currents that made closing with hostile ships difficult – could still be attacked in this manner.

The typical Viking bow was not excessively powerful, with a draw weight of 36–45kg (80–100lbs). This would give an effective range of perhaps 200m (656ft), and someone who regularly used the bow for hunting would be able to hit a man at a reasonable proportion of this distance. It is likely that most Viking bows were of fairly simple construction, with a curved stave about 2m (6.5ft) long or a little less, made of yew, elm or ash wood. It has been suggested that the Vikings may have made use of recurve bows or composite bows that included horn as

ABOVE: **The spear could be cast, but it was more often used in the hand. An overhand thrust was powerful and gave the wielder a reach advantage over someone armed with a sax or short-handled axe. Spears could also be used at close quarters by a skilled warrior.**

ABOVE: **The Vikings did not deploy a corps of specialist archers in their forces. Anyone who had a bow and was skilled in its use would loose a few shots at the enemy before closing for hand-to-hand combat with his fellows.**

well as wood, but these cannot have been common if they were used at all.

Fighting Techniques

The typical Viking warrior, as already noted, was not a professional fighting-man, but would have received some instruction at arms while growing up. He would also have hunted and played manly games such as wrestling, and had a strong fighting spirit. He may or may not have possessed a helmet; armour is less likely.

The probable arms for most warriors engaged in a raid or feud would be a spear and shield, plus an axe or sax for close combat. Some men might sling their shields on their back to use their spears two-handed, but once close combat ensued the majority would fight protected by a shield.

Techniques for fighting with sword and shield, and axe and shield, were quite similar (and thus apply also to the sax). The usual method was to close in, covered by an attack that would force the opponent onto the defensive, to deliver a series of aggressive strikes and blows, and then to break contact and get ready for another exchange. If the opponent was downed the warrior would move on to another target; if not, he might fight a series of such engagements with the same foe until the tides of battle swept them apart.

Rapid movement and aggression were an important part of the Viking fighting style, and in many ways served as a good defence. An opponent who quailed in the face of extreme aggression could be easily killed, and even a more resolute man who was forced to concentrate on defence was at a severe disadvantage. The attacker, once he gained the initiative in this manner, could choose when and where to strike, and had a better chance of getting through his opponent's defences.

Fighting in short exchanges and then breaking off allowed a fighter to get his breath back, to see what was going on and to assist friends who were in trouble. It also reduced the chances that he would be flanked or hit from behind by an opportunistic opponent and allowed him to move to prevent this happening to friends who were hotly engaged.

Sword and axe blows tended to be downward, either more or less straight down at the head or diagonally at the shoulders and neck. Such strikes had the advantage of gravity assisting the power of the blow, and were more common than upward cuts. Horizontal blows were also delivered, generally at the body.

Cuts to the legs seem to have been a very common tactic. This was probably due to the prevalence of shields and helmets, which made body and head cuts difficult. The attacker's shield also influenced where he could cut; the logical counter to an overhead cut was to raise the shield to defend and launch a cut of your own to a lower target.

Hand to Hand

Getting past the shield was, to a great extent, the essence of Viking hand-to-hand combat. One method might be to batter it to pieces with heavy blows, but this was time consuming and labour intensive. A more effective measure was to get the opponent to move it out of the way. A sword thrust to the face

LEFT: The axe or halberd blade in the foreground of this display would not have existed at the start of the Viking Age, but weapons technology did advance and new construction techniques came into use as time went by.

could be used to draw the opponent's shield upwards, opening him up for a leg cut. Alternatively, a warrior armed with an axe could use the shield against its owner by hooking it and pulling with the blade, and a swordsman could use the pommel of his sword as a hook. A sharp yank would drag the shield user out of position and expose him to a blow.

One effective variant on this technique was to hook the shield, pull the user forward and thrust the axe haft at his face. Although it had no point, the haft would strike a painful blow even if the horns of the blade did not cut the opponent. He would likely recoil from the strike and be off balance as the axe-man followed up. Axes could also be used to hook the opponent's leg, arm or head. Longer-hafted weapons were ideal for this, and could be used to drag or trip as necessary.

Two-handed weapons such as large axes were likely to smash right through a shield that was wielded in an unskilled manner. Merely holding it up would not suffice; a two-handed axe blow would destroy most shields. However, by moving inside the arc of the strike the shield could be used to stop the haft of the weapon, placing the axe-man at a huge disadvantage against his opponent's shorter weapon. Spear thrusts could be deflected in the same way, pushing the point aside with the shield and thus opening up the spearman for a counterattack.

Another way to deal with a spear attack was to leap over it or jump up and land on the haft, breaking it; alternatively, it was possible to break it by striking it with a sword. Some spears had iron protection on the haft to reduce the chances of this happening, but this would not prevent the weapon from being hooked with an axe blade or sword pommel and dragged aside.

BELOW: A Viking force was not a drilled military unit but a group of individual warriors armed with a mix of swords, axes and spears. The Vikings were at their best in a confused melee where skill, ferocity and loose but effective cooperation were the dominant factors.

Mobility was very important to the warrior armed with a two-handed weapon. If he allowed his opponent to get too close he might find himself at a major disadvantage. Axes, in particular, had an optimum striking range; too close and the wielder might not be able to deliver a proper stroke. He might also find his weapon seized, pushed against him with a shield bind or similarly controlled. An opponent armed with a sword, sax or even a knife had an advantage in such a situation, but if the warrior could keep the distance open he could choose when to strike and force his opponent to move through a killing zone if he wanted to close in and attack.

> 'IF A MAN'S TIME HAS NOT COME, SOMETHING WILL SAVE HIM.'

Wrestling

Other techniques were used as necessary. Warriors are recorded in the sagas as throwing stones for lack of better weapons, or tossing aside their weapons to grapple with an opponent. A skilled wrestler could negate any advantage an opponent might have in terms of armour, shield and weapons by closing in and taking him to the ground, or throwing him down onto a rock.

A knife could be used in grappling, and although mail would be useful in protecting the wearer, if the knife wielder were a skilled wrestler he would be able to make an opportunity for a killing thrust, immobilizing his opponent's defending limbs and finding a location uncovered by armour. Alternatively, improvised weapons such as sword hilts and rocks that lay to hand could be used to strike an opponent during a grapple, or more sophisticated techniques intended to choke or break limbs might be applied.

Many Vikings would have known how to wrestle as this was one of their sports as well as something that young men were expected to learn. There were basically three types of wrestling: glima was all about skill and technique; freestyle wrestling was looser; and there was also a 'style' referred to as 'crude' wrestling, which was a sort of 'anything-goes, all-in' combat. A battlefield grapple would resemble this style the most, with any dirty trick used to ensure victory and thus survival.

ABOVE: **This carving depicts a capability credited to the berserkers – the ability to throw two spears simultaneously. This feat has been replicated by modern re-enactors and is effective, but it requires a great deal of effort to learn and may have contributed to their reputation for supernatural talents.**

Although most Vikings, even those engaged in a raid, were not professional warriors, many would have received some training and gained experience on previous expeditions. A few would have been professionals in the service of Jarls or kings, who would have the very best arms and equipment. They would also train and fight full-time, and would be among the most dangerous opponents anyone would have to face.

The Berserkers

The most notorious and controversial Viking warriors were the *berserkers*. The word conjures up a popular image of howling crazy-men, possibly naked, who would kill everything in sight at the slightest provocation. This was probably not the case, although the word berserker seems to be applied differently in various sagas, so perhaps there was more than one type.

Various explanations have been put forward for the origins of the word 'berserker'. Some have suggested that it means 'bare of shirt' or 'bare-chested'. Although the idea that berserkers fought naked has long been discredited, it could be that the word referred to a warrior who fought without the protection of a mail-shirt. A variant on this is the idea that these men did not use shields in battle. The word could also mean 'bear cloak' or 'bear shirt', and may refer to the bearskin cloaks that some elite warriors were given.

The insane fury of the berserkers is legendary but its origins are unclear. It is possible that it was chemically induced, by hallucinogenic mushrooms or an excess of alcohol, or that it represented a dissociative personality disorder similar to that which causes some people to run amok in other cultures. The act of entering the famous furious rage, 'going berserk', was known as *berserkergang*.

One reasonably plausible explanation is that the original berserkers were elite warriors who fought with great aggression and little regard for their own safety. A certain kind of man joins such a group, and some of them may have been prone to dissociative behaviour triggered by the stress of battle. This could result in the murderous fury that berserkers are known for, and their habit of attacking both sides with equal enthusiasm.

Over time the entire elite body of men became associated with the behaviour of some of its members, and the concept of the berserker as an elite, highly skilled and very aggressive warrior became conflated with the idea of a frothing psychopath. It is possible that the berserkers themselves played upon this image to frighten prospective enemies, and that saga-poets contributed to their legend. By the end of the Viking period berserkers were known for their insane ferocity and also a range of supernatural feats, including the ability to blunt a sword by casting a spell on it.

To many observers, the ability of an aggressive, highly trained and well-protected warrior to demolish several opponents in quick succession might have seemed supernatural. Tales of the berserkers' abilities may have been inflated in the way that those of some modern martial artists have been. Today, there are plenty of people willing to believe that some martial artists can kill with a touch or knock a man out without laying a hand on him, despite the fact that this is obvious nonsense, and we live in a distinctly sceptical age. The people of the Viking Age were more open to such concepts.

Thus it is likely that the berserkers were indeed a band of highly skilled warriors who fought with great ferocity and extreme aggression, but the proportion of them who were genuinely insane may have been fairly small. It is not difficult to believe that in a time when the gods were believed to walk the earth, a band of warriors that included a proportion of genuine psychopaths gained a reputation for supernatural ferocity and were credited with abilities far beyond the norm.

BELOW: An eleventh century elk horn carving of a Viking warrior found at Sigtuna in Sweden. The helmet has a pronounced nasal bar but no sign of anything resembling horns.

7

EXPLORATION, SETTLEMENT AND TRADE

The Vikings were great explorers. They voyaged as far as the Americas and set up settlements in what is now Canada, long before the 'discovery' of the continent by European explorers. They also sailed around the European coast and into the Mediterranean and pushed down the Russian rivers to the Black Sea.

That the Vikings managed these incredible voyages is remarkable enough, but that they did so in an open-topped ship propelled by oars and a fairly primitive sail suggests they must have been extraordinarily hardy and brave. Of course, we know that they were exactly that.

Courage and strength on the oars can only do so much, however. Many of the Vikings' voyages followed the coast or the path of a river, which made navigation reasonably simple. To cross open water, out of sight of land, required some form of navigation system. It would be centuries before the sextant was invented, and the magnetic compass was at that time unknown

OPPOSITE: **Although the sailing rig used by the Vikings was simple, it was sufficient for long voyages on the open sea. Such a small vessel must have been a frightening place to be in bad weather.**

ABOVE: **The sagas suggest that the Vikings used the polarizing properties of naturally occurring crystals to determine the position of the sun, even on an overcast day.**

in Europe, yet the Vikings managed to navigate somehow.

It is possible that some expeditions simply set sail and trusted the gods, but since ships reliably made long-distance voyages a more scientific system must have been available. There is some debate as to exactly what this might have been. The position of the sun at certain times of day offers one reasonable explanation, but this would only work when the sun's position was visible.

Sunstones and Sailing Rigs

Some of the sagas mention the use of a semi-transparent 'sunstone', through which the sky was viewed. This was probably a naturally-occurring crystal of cordierite, which changes colour when rotated as polarized light is viewed through it. Although humans cannot see it, sunlight is polarized by the Earth's atmosphere in a direction at right angles to the Sun's location. Some insects and birds can see this effect and use it to navigate; perhaps the Vikings did too.

From the polarization of the light passing through the sun stone it was possible to determine the location of the sun even if it was not visible. Any patch of clear sky, or even thin cloud, could be used. Once the location of the sun was known, directions could be calculated. This method was not infallible – Iceland was most likely first discovered by a vessel bound for the Faroe Islands that went off course – but it served to get a ship across open water and into sight of a coast that could then be followed until familiar landmarks were sighted.

Water had provided the Norsemen with a means of transport and communication since long before the Viking Age, but one factor that enabled long-range exploration was the development of ships with a sailing rig. Although relatively basic, a sail reduced crew fatigue and permitted rest during a long voyage. Oars could still be used for long distances, however, with the crew operating in shifts. Other tasks were shared out as necessary, with everyone on board taking turns at various jobs. There was

no real distinction between passengers and crew, other than
when someone paid money to be exempted from duties.

The early Viking boats allowed them to cross the Baltic
and to conduct expeditions of raiding and trade between their
homelands of Denmark, Norway and Sweden. Better ships
allowed them to strike out across the North Sea for England,
or to follow the coasts around to Aquitaine and beyond.

Settlers

Vikings began to settle in the islands between Scandinavia and
Scotland from around 820 AD, and probably earlier. The islands
were in many ways similar to the Vikings' homeland, and offered a
place to set up a new home for those who wanted or needed one.
By 875 AD, numerous Vikings had moved to the islands to escape
Harald Fine-Hair's attempt to unify Norway and were living
in what are now the Scottish islands, including the Faroes, the
Orkney and Shetland Islands, the Hebrides and the Isle of Man.

This pattern of settling the islands rather than the mainland
– although it is possible that some groups did penetrate the
mainland – reflects the Vikings' seagoing nature. They had

BELOW: **The remains of
a longhouse in the Faroe
Islands, dating from the
tenth century.**

OPPOSITE: **The southern reaches of Greenland were far more habitable in the Viking Age than they are today. The cooling climate eventually made the seas impassable to longships.**

arrived in the islands as explorers and used the sea to remain connected with their kin elsewhere. They were not trying to create a great nation, simply taking suitable land where they found it. Opposition was far less in the islands than on the mainland, where the Picts and other groups already had much of the useable land and were capable of fighting to defend it.

These early settlers were, therefore, not colonists as such; the era of large-scale Viking settlement was yet to come. But settle they did, bringing their traditional way of life with them and using their new island homes as a base for further exploration, trade or raids. It may well have been Vikings from the Orkney Isles who plundered Lindisfarne in 793 AD and Iona in 794 AD.

Iceland and Greenland

Exploration continued, with ever more daring expeditions pushing farther out into the unknown reaches of the Atlantic Ocean. Some of these expeditions will have found nothing but open sea, of course. Others will have been lost at sea, and in many cases what an expedition found may not have been recorded. Thus it is possible that the Vikings had already known about Iceland since a man named Naddod 'discovered' it around 860 AD.

Naddod was an early settler in the Faroes, and is credited with accidentally discovering Iceland when his ship went off course and became lost. According to some sources there were

RIGHT: **Off course and far from known waters, Naddod sights land – which turns out to be Iceland – around 860 AD.**

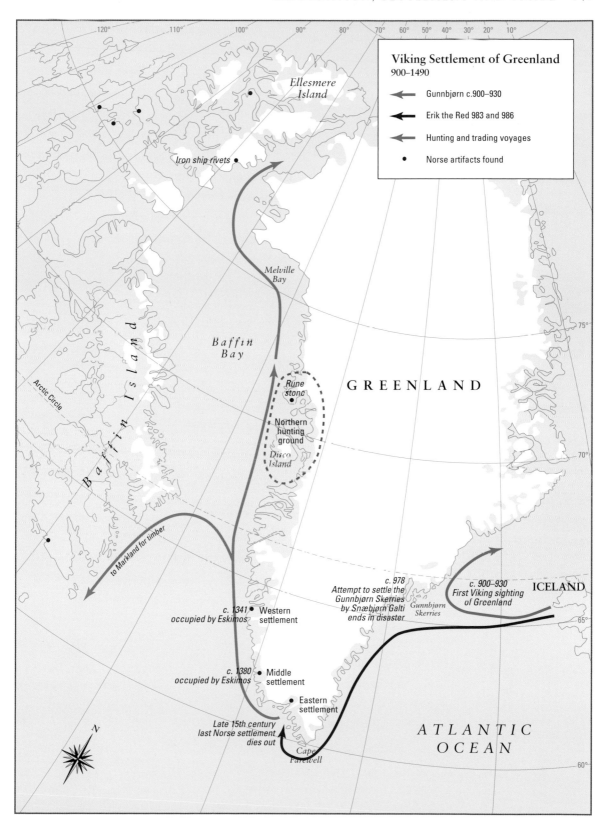

120° 110° 100° 90° 80° 70° 60° 50° 40° 30° 20° 10°

Viking Settlement of Greenland
900–1490

→ Gunnbjørn c.900–930

→ Erik the Red 983 and 986

→ Hunting and trading voyages

• Norse artifacts found

Ellesmere Island

Iron ship rivets

Melville Bay

Baffin Island

Baffin Bay

Arctic Circle

Rune stone

Northern hunting ground

Disco Island

GREENLAND

75°

70°

to Markland for timber

c. 978
Attempt to settle the Gunnbjørn Skerries by Snæbjørn Galti ends in disaster

Gunnbjørn Skerries

c. 900–930
First Viking sighting of Greenland

ICELAND

c. 1341
occupied by Eskimos • Western settlement

c. 1380
occupied by Eskimos • Middle settlement

• Eastern settlement

65°

Late 15th century
last Norse settlement
dies out

Cape Farewell

ATLANTIC
OCEAN

60°

N

ABOVE: **Erik the Red may have undertaken the exploration of Greenland for lack of anywhere else to go. His talent for getting himself outlawed led to the establishment of a small colony with Erik as First Settler.**

already people living in Iceland when the first Vikings arrived. They were monks from Ireland who left when the Norsemen started moving in. There is some evidence that this may have been the case, but if it is true, then the population was simply a small group living in one location and not a large-scale settlement.

The climate was milder at the time the Vikings arrived in Iceland, but the first of them to spend a winter in Iceland did so in a very cold year. The name Iceland was inspired by drift ice floating on the sea just offshore. However, Iceland was desirable enough real estate that some of the explorers reported that every blade of grass dripped with butter. Soon, settlers began to arrive. The first of them was Ingolf Arnarson, and many others followed.

By 870 AD Iceland had at least a few permanent settlements, and within half a century the population was perhaps 50,000–60,000 people occupying all the usable land. In the meantime Iceland became the jumping-off point for further exploration westward. Around 930 AD, an Icelandic seafarer named Gunnbjørn Ulf-Krakason was blown off course by a storm and sighted land to the west. He did not land there, and there are no records of anyone else venturing ashore in this new world until around 980 AD, when Erik the Red launched an expedition.

Erik the Red may have acquired his name from bloody deeds. He had left his native Norway to escape a feud or blood vengeance, but was outlawed not long after trying to settle in Iceland. Erik's outlawry was for a fixed term; his exploration of the land to the west coincides with the three-year period of banishment customary in such cases. He returned to Iceland, but it seems that he was soon outlawed again. He led a new expedition to the land he had discovered, naming it Greenland, and settled there.

As already noted, the climate was milder at that time than it is now, and Greenland may well have merited the name.

Certainly the southern tip, where Erik settled, was entirely habitable. However, it lacked timber for shipbuilding and other construction, and as the population grew it became desirable to seek a source closer than Scandinavia or the Scottish Isles.

America, Europe and Russia

The discovery of America was probably first made by Bjarni Herjolfsson, whose parents were among the settlers who went with Erik the Red. This came as a surprise to Bjarni, who was at the time an adult and had been in Norway when his parents departed Iceland. He attempted to go to Greenland to join them, but was blown far off course by a storm. Sighting land, he decided to investigate even though he was sure it was not Greenland. Bjarni sailed close to the shore but did not land.

Having assured himself that this was indeed not his intended destination, Bjarni sailed for Greenland and there told of what he had seen. One of the sons of Erik the Red, Leif Eriksson, was the first Viking to land in the Americas, leading an expedition to explore this new land. He ascertained that it had timber, and plans were made for a settlement.

In the meantime, Viking expeditions had been moving out in other directions. Russia was accessible by land via what is now

BELOW: Leif, son of Erik The Red, pushed the boundaries of Viking exploration as far west as they would ever go when he landed in the Americas.

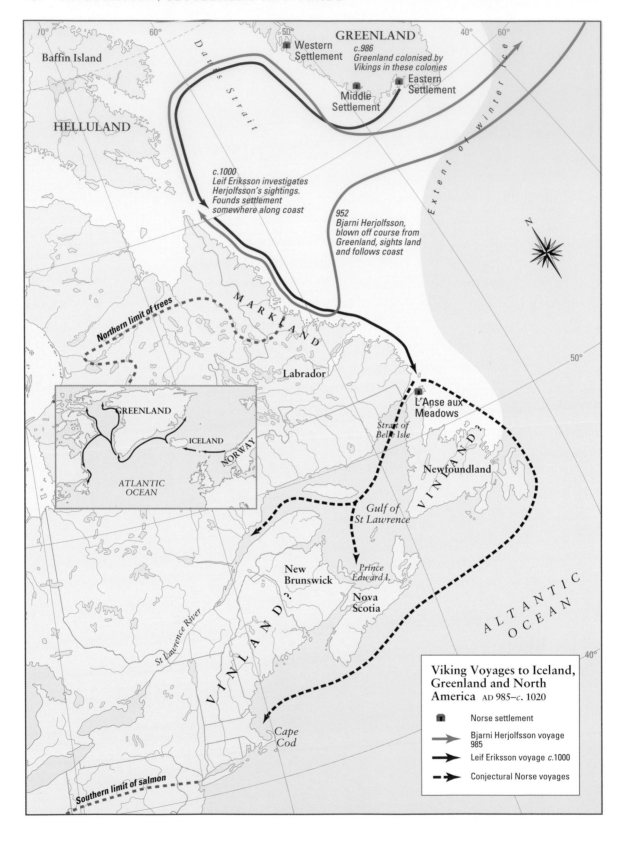

70°

60°

50°

GREENLAND

Baffin Island

■ Western
Settlement

c.986
Greenland colonised by
Vikings in these colonies

40°

60°

HELLULAND

■ Middle
Settlement

■ Eastern
Settlement

Davis Strait

Extent of winter ice

c.1000
Leif Eriksson investigates
Herjolfsson's sightings.
Founds settlement
somewhere along coast

952
Bjarni Herjolfsson,
blown off course from
Greenland, sights land
and follows coast

N

M A R K L A N D

Labrador

50°

L'Anse aux
Meadows

Strait of
Belle Isle

GREENLAND

ICELAND

NORWAY

ATLANTIC
OCEAN

V I N L A N D

Newfoundland

Gulf of
St Lawrence

Prince
Edward I.

**New
Brunswick**
?

**Nova
Scotia**

A L T A N T I C
OCEAN

St Lawrence River

V I N L A N D

40°

Cape
Cod

Southern limit of salmon

Northern limit of trees

**Viking Voyages to Iceland,
Greenland and North
America** AD 985–*c.* 1020

■   Norse settlement

→   Bjarni Herjolfsson voyage
985

→   Leif Eriksson voyage *c.*1000

▸ ▸ ▸   Conjectural Norse voyages

Finland, and northern Europe could be reached through southern Denmark. The Baltic and the southern coasts of the North Sea gave access to more of Europe. Contact, especially by way of land borders, had been ongoing for centuries. Viking expeditions gradually became more ambitious, eventually establishing fairly regular contact with Constantinople and even Baghdad.

'WHO TRAVELS WIDELY NEEDS HIS WITS ABOUT HIM, THE STUPID SHOULD STAY AT HOME.'

Rivers were the key to long-distance travel for Viking explorers and traders. From the eastern end of the Baltic Sea, what is now the Gulf of Finland, the River Neva offered easy access to Lake Ladoga and then on to Lake Onega. From there it was possible to reach the River Volga, which could be navigated all the way to the Caspian Sea, albeit with some difficulty. Tributaries of the Volga gave access to a wide area.

Viking expeditions pushed up the Volga, and people of Scandinavian origin were living among the local population from 750 AD or perhaps earlier. Some were traders, some were effectively mercenaries and some were simply craftsmen and farmers who had relocated for whatever reason. There have been claims that many important cities in Russia were founded by Vikings, although controversy continues to rage over this issue.

It is known that in some areas Scandinavian men were known as 'Rus', but whether this was because what is now Russia was largely populated or at least ruled by Scandinavians, or because distant people did not really know the difference between a native of Russia and a Scandinavian, remains open to question. What is known is that Viking settlements around Lake Ladoga existed from the beginning of the Viking Age, and smaller groups lived further into Russia. Trade expeditions from this region ranged far and wide, wherever a great river gave them access.

The other major Viking trade route across Europe was down the Dnieper River, leading eventually to the Black Sea. Along this route were several settlements that expanded into great cities, Kiev and Novgorod among them. Viking influences were at play in the development of these cities, and in some cases a Viking leader is credited with founding them.

OPPOSITE: Exploration of the New World was undertaken by just a handful of ships, and was never more than cursory. It is not certain exactly how far the Vikings penetrated inland, nor exactly where they landed.

The internal European route, trading down the Oder, offered additional possibilities. From here it was possible to connect with the overland Mainz–Cracow–Kiev trade route, or to join the Danube and then gain access to the Black Sea. The Black Sea, of course, connected to the Mediterranean, making it possible to trade for goods from North Africa.

Overcoming Obstacles

The major rivers of Europe made all of this possible, although not without a great deal of effort. Navigating a great river was easy at times, where an oar-powered ship could move steadily along through reasonably deep water. However, there were rapids and shallows to negotiate. A less intrepid race than the Norsemen might have been discouraged by the difficulties of passing these obstacles, but the Vikings overcame them in one of two ways.

Sometimes it was possible to work the ship carefully through, with men at the prow using poles to test the depth of the water and push off the ship from dangerous rocks. Alternatively, the ship could be unloaded and portaged around an obstacle. Methods of portage varied: a smallish boat could be picked up and carried by the crew, while a larger vessel had to be dragged. Portage was also used to move ships overland from one river to another if no suitable water link was available. The cargo then had to be brought up and reloaded, after which the ship could set out on the next stage of the journey. Portage was, however, not without risk. Not only could the ship be damaged or crewmembers injured, but portage-sites were also a good spot to attack trade ships.

Outposts and forts were built to protect or control important portages, both by Vikings and by the local population. By controlling these choke points, a king or other leader could generate revenue by forcing traders to pay a toll, or protect his own trade interests by making sure that ships were not ambushed. Many of these portage-site forts grew into towns that became important trading sites in their own right. The Viking traders gave names to the portages that they had to negotiate, many of which are still in common use

BELOW: **A tenth century Viking-style cloak fastener found near Smolensk, Russia. Such items were traded and copied by local craftsmen, so all that can be inferred from such finds is Viking influence, not necessarily major settlement.**

LEFT: A small boat could be picked up and carried overland, from one waterway to another. Moving something as large as a longship was rather more involved and time-consuming, and could make an expedition vulnerable to attack.

today. The Dnieper, for example, has seven major rapids, most of which have Scandinavian names. Perhaps the locals called them something different, but it is the Viking names that have passed into history. There are many reasons why this might happen, but the most likely is the fact that the Viking traders interacted with many people over a wide area, and told other prospective expedition members about the hazards of the route they planned to take. Their names for various features would become far more widespread than those used by the local population.

Overland Trade

Viking trade also went overland, away from the rivers and their tributaries. Overland travel was possible for a considerable distance, although in most cases expeditions did not go far beyond the places a ship could reach. One exception to this was the overland connection to the Silk Road. Leaving the Volga where it turned south, traders could make a hazardous crossing of the desert and eventually join the Silk Road near the Aral Sea. From there it was possible to reach Baghdad fairly easily, and to get access to foreign goods coming all the way from China.

It is not clear whether Viking traders pushed to the Far East along the Silk Road, but it is probably unlikely. Coins and other goods from various places on the route, and from the Arabic world, have been found in Scandinavia, but it is more likely

ABOVE: Trade, such as silver to make this bracelet, came into Viking lands from far afield. Some items were directly obtained by expeditions, while other goods passed through several hands during their long journey.

that they came from trade in Baghdad or Constantinople than from expeditions along the Silk Road. However, the Vikings were an adventurous lot and it is not impossible that an expedition proceeded very far eastwards.

Most of the traders who took part in these expeditions were not merchants at all, but farmers or craftsmen who wanted to ensure that the supplies they obtained met their needs. An expedition could take a man away from home for a long time – it was common to sail to Iceland from Scandinavia one year and stay over the winter months before returning home when better weather returned. Nevertheless, the proceeds of a successful expedition made it worthwhile as long as the trader's land or business was looked after in his absence.

Specialist merchants did exist and many Jarls undertook trading expeditions in search of profits. Others made money off trade in different ways, for example by controlling key points on a trade route or by ensuring that traders conducted their business in the Jarl's territory and not that of a rival. It was trade that caused the first towns to be constructed; the Viking way of life was fairly dispersed and a concentrated, urbanized population was, up to that point, not considered desirable.

Trade Towns

Urbanization might not have been particularly desirable to many Vikings who lived in the trade towns. Conditions were less healthy than on the dispersed farmsteads, and the way of life was different. But the trade towns were necessary. They appeared in obvious, logical locations with good access by land, water or both, and were sometimes protected by fortifications in the form of a ditch, earth rampart and wooden palisade.

The trade towns were not large by modern or even medieval standards, with a population of fewer than 1000 individuals, but they still represented an unusual concentration of people. A larger proportion of the populace were specialists such as swordsmiths than was typical on the farmsteads. Working in a trade town gave the craftsman access to materials that came in from trade and also a wider market for his goods. The prosperity of a town also meant that more people had spare money to buy non-essential goods, and the central location meant that they could do so without travelling to a remote farmstead to buy from a renowned craftsman.

'THE REASON WHY YOUNG MEN GET NOWHERE IS THAT THEY OVERESTIMATE THE OBSTACLES EVERY TIME.'

The politics of trade were complex and could be bloody at times. Disputes over trade or raids against expeditions passing through the region were not the only hazard; Jarls might find themselves at odds over control of trade. This was generally achieved by creating favourable conditions and a suitable venue. The former meant relative stability and the rule of law, along with ways to make the traders' lives easier. This included laws that required local residents to assist with beaching ships for the winter and other heavy tasks.

A suitable trade town was the best guarantee that a king or Jarl would benefit from trade within his lands. In 808 AD, Godfred, a Danish king, founded the trade town of Hedeby. The expense was no doubt considerable but the investment repaid itself many times over. With access to both the Baltic sea trade and overland traffic, Hedeby became a trade centre known to merchants in far-off Constantinople. By attracting trade, Godfred not only ensured that he had access to the goods sold there, but he also benefited from taxes and fees paid by the merchants.

Coin and Silver

Much trade was done by barter, but silver was a preferred medium and minted coins were used. Another medium of exchange was hack-silver. This was silver that had previously been used for jewellery, tableware or any other purpose but was currently in use as currency. Its condition was irrelevant – hack-silver was often made up of damaged items – all that mattered was its weight. The term hack-silver comes from the practice of chopping up silver items for use in this manner.

The name of the Russian Ruble comes from a word meaning 'to chop', so the Russian currency may have gained its name from the practice of chopping up any available pieces of silver to create a sufficient weight to pay for goods. Silver rods were also used, often quite crudely formed into a shape that was less awkward to carry than assorted silver objects and was easy to cut up. Rods required much less effort to create than coins and they served the same purpose.

As the value of hack-silver was based on its weight a trader needed to carry a set of scales. Coins were also weighed to determine their value. At other times this was to determine whether silver coins had been debased with metal of lesser value, but in the Viking Age it was also necessary because many traders would chop bits off their coins like any other pieces of hack-silver. A coin's value was determined by its weight. Coinage was not representative in that time; its worth was intrinsic and absolute.

The amount of silver flowing into the Viking world was very considerable, and not all of it came from trade. Some came from what amounted to an extortion racket, whereby kingdoms

BELOW: **A reconstructed Viking settlement at Hedeby on the Jutland Peninsula. Most settlements were small farming communities inhabited by an extended family, plus a few workers and/or slaves.**

LEFT: Minted coins were useful in commerce, especially in trade-towns like Hedeby, but they were still treated like hack-silver in many quarters, with chunks chopped off to make up a necessary weight of silver.

wishing to buy a period of peace with the Vikings paid a fee termed Danegeld. This was essentially protection money; tribute paid to Viking kings to prevent their people from raiding. Danegeld only worked when kings could control their people effectively; a kingdom that was raided too heavily and too soon after paying Danegeld would not pay again, but when the system worked it was extremely lucrative.

Danegeld provided Viking overlords with a huge income and also freed up their fighting men for other tasks, including raids on those who preferred to take their chances. Since the Vikings were farmers, raiders and traders on a more or less interchangeable basis, Danegeld contributed to further prosperity by freeing men who would otherwise have been out raiding to work their land or undertake trading expeditions.

Mixed Goods

The goods that were traded within the Viking lands sometimes came from very far afield, but were generally fairly local. Different regions were known for producing certain goods. Food, furs, homespun cloth and the like were of course made, grown or hunted more or less everywhere, but some items could only be obtained by trade. Walrus ivory came from Greenland, and tin and linen from the British Isles. The main source of good iron was Sweden, while timber for shipbuilding was mainly obtained from Norway.

Some specialist goods came from outside the Viking world. Glass and some finely made weapons came from the Frankish kingdoms of Europe; silk came by way of Constantinople. Much of the silver in circulation also came in via the river trade from the Arabic world, although later in the Viking Age European

ABOVE: **Viking traders dealt in slaves like many other merchants of the time. The buyer in this case is Persian, suggesting that the slave-girl will end up a long way from home.**

mines provided the majority. Slaves could be obtained anywhere, although it appears from some sources that Russia and Eastern Europe were the main providers.

Violence for Sale

One of the major exports of the Viking kingdoms was violence, and not just in the form of raiding expeditions. Viking warriors served as bodyguards, mercenaries and members of the personal forces of rulers all over Europe and the Mediterranean. In many cases this was a personal and ad hoc arrangement, whereby a man skilled at arms and combat, and possessing his own weapons, would offer his service to a prospective employer in return for pay and board.

Some of these mercenaries were very loyal. Viking culture was one in which loyalty was freely given by a warrior and was returned by the lord. A Jarl or king who mistreated his warriors or failed to hold them in sufficient regard might find they transferred their loyalty elsewhere – if he was lucky. Bloody vengeance for a slight was not uncommon. However, a lord who treated his men well and fairly, and who showed himself to be worthy of their company, would find them to be loyal.

Culture was not much of a barrier to the Viking mercenary. He would serve a foreign king who treated him well and paid him fairly. Gifts, such as a sword, would help cement loyalty so long as they were not seen as an attempt simply to buy him. Gestures such as honouring a man's deeds at a feast or merely offering a few words of praise when deserved were also important for maintaining Viking loyalty.

Pay was also necessary. A man who was well treated by his lord would put up with a lot, but there was a limit. The warrior Halldor Snorrason is recorded as being offended by his pay, which was given in coins so debased that their silver content was little over 30 per cent, as opposed to the usual 90 per cent. As well as the obvious financial drawbacks this suggested that he was not valued highly, and the offended Halldor threw the coins to the floor. He more or less threatened to quit, saying that since he was not paid in real money he was not willing to serve, and his king got the point. Halldor's pay was in pure silver thereafter and, presumably, his working relationship with his employer was restored.

'ONLY A COWARD WAITS TO BE TAKEN LIKE A LAMB FROM THE FOLD OR A FOX FROM A TRAP.'

The Varangian Guard

The most famous Viking mercenaries were the Varangian Guard, who served the Byzantine Emperor. The guard was formed in 988 AD from men recruited in Kievan Rus, when 6000 of them were sent by Vladimir I of Kiev to fulfil treaty obligations granting assistance to Emperor Basil II. These troops distinguished themselves in battle – and afterwards, with enthusiastic pursuit of their beaten foe – and the guard was retained in service.

Varangians had been serving the Byzantine emperors for at least half a century by that point, although not in a large and clearly identified elite unit. The term 'Varangians' was in use at the time to refer to the people of the state of Rus, and more specifically to their ruling class, who included many Vikings. It was also applied, somewhat vaguely, to any Viking or indeed anyone who seemed generally Scandinavian or north European.

To many, the words 'Viking' and 'Varangian' were synonymous, although the usage varied.

There were Varangians in Byzantine service as early as 911 AD, and possibly before. Their name for the region was as vague as the one applied to them; they referred to the Byzantine Empire as 'Greece'. Thus, a warrior who was 'in Greece' could actually be anywhere within the Byzantine Empire or just beyond it, and might therefore be serving the emperor or just in the general area. This makes some apparently precise records quite misleading; it is as difficult to determine exactly where a Viking who was 'in Greece' was and what he was doing as it is to pin down the origins of any given 'Varangian'.

It is known that the Varangian Guard, whose men were of Rus Viking origin and were dressed, armed and fought in the Viking manner, fought in the service of several Byzantine emperors and earned great distinction. Coming from outside the Byzantine Empire, they were – at least, at first – less likely to become involved in palace politics and the endless plots that wracked the Empire.

Although the Varangians were later assimilated into local culture and became accessible to those with a mind to involve them in plots, they retained their reputation for unswerving loyalty. This was likely the result of cultural traditions and pride in their regiment, whose customs derived from Viking warrior culture. Honour and loyalty were vitally important to a warrior, and he would not turn on his master for mere promises of pay. A valid comparison is the Roman Praetorian Guard, which was notorious not only as a pawn in the game of politics but

ABOVE: A depiction of the Varangians in service with Basil II, in 1014 AD. The Varangian Guard long outlived the Viking era, retaining its unique identity despite recruiting from a variety of sources.

also as a powerful player. Roman emperors were deposed by the Praetorians who were supposed to defend them, sometimes for no better reason than the emperor had not been sufficiently generous in bribing them. Not so the Varangians, who for the most part stood above local politics.

Shifting Loyalties

This reliability was not quite so absolute as it seems at first glance, however. On one occasion the Varangian Guard decided that its loyalty was to the throne rather than the emperor, and participated in a coup. Varangians also mutinied on another occasion, and were so renowned for drunkenness that they were at times known as 'the emperor's wineskins'.

The Varangian Guard was highly valued and enjoyed the right to plunder its own palace upon the death of an emperor. Each Varangian was entitled to go to the treasury and carry off as much as he could take with him. For many this was a severance bonus and they would return home afterwards, although others took service with the new emperor.

Service to any given emperor ended at the moment of his death. For example, the Varangian Guard was marginally too late to prevent the murder of Emperor Nikephoros II at the hands of John Tzimiskes. Arriving to find their charge dead and his killer standing over him, the Varangian Guard transferred its loyalty to Tzimizekes and was ready to defend him as the new emperor – just as soon as its men had finished raiding the treasury.

The Varangians had their foibles and a tendency to be uncouth and brawl or drink, but their loyalty and their potency on the battlefield was extremely valuable. They were widely referred to as 'axe-wielding barbarians' and earned a fearsome reputation for being quite capable of chopping their way through the enemy lines. They were not invincible, of course, and some of their more notable defeats were at the hands of Normans of the same Viking stock.

BELOW: **The aggressive tactics and simple but effective weaponry of the Varangian Guard proved extremely effective in combat, earning the guard its reputation as the elite of the Byzantine forces.**

Service in the Varangian Guard was highly desirable for a young Viking wanting to make a name for himself. Large numbers of hopefuls made their way to 'Greece' seeking employment; so many, in fact, that not all could be given a place. Those denied entry to the guard usually took other military service, flooding the region with warriors. This exodus of young men was of such concern to kings in Viking lands that measures were taken to try to reduce their numbers.

Laws were passed prohibiting a man from inheriting while he was 'in Greece', ensuring that at the least he returned home to claim his birthright. Having left Varangian service and made the long journey home, it was to be hoped that he would stay. The prohibition might have deterred some, but not enough to weaken the guard.

Some prominent Vikings served in the Varangian Guard, of whom the most notable is Harald Hardrada who became the King of Norway. Harald's death in 1066 AD marked what is normally considered to be the end of the Viking Age, but the Varangian Guard continued long afterwards. It recruited people from traditionally Viking lands such as Danes, and also those from Viking-influenced areas such as England. By the 1400s the Viking Age was long over, but one of its legacies – the famed Varangian Guard – still existed in a recognizable form.

BELOW: Emperor Nikephoros II was an effective military commander, but this did not prevent his assassination by his nephew, John Tzimiskes. The Varangian Guard swore allegiance to the assassin rather than taking vengeance.

Viking Ships and Transport

It has been suggested that improvements in shipbuilding were among the factors that propelled the Vikings from local significance onto the world stage. Certainly, none of the trading, exploration or raiding expeditions undertaken by the Vikings would have been possible without a high standard of shipbuilding expertise. This was gained over many decades, first producing small boats and then increasingly large ships capable of withstanding the conditions of harsh northern waters.

LEFT: The Varangian Guard distinguished itself during the sieges of Constantinople in 1203 and 1204 AD, but were ultimately unable to prevent the capture of the city. The Byzantine Empire was so crippled by internal politics that its fall had become inevitable.

Several types of boat and ship were used, although it may have been hard for observers to tell them apart. Small boats such as the four-oared *feraeringr* were obviously utility craft, but the somewhat larger *karfi* was used for various tasks in coastal waters, including serving as a warship when necessary. There were no special requirements for a warship at the time – it did not mount a ram or other weapons, for example – so any fast and easily handled vessel could be effectively used in combat.

Smallish coastal vessels were designed for short trips within sight of land, and could run up on the shore to escape bad weather. They typically had a well in the centre, around the mast, for cargo. The fore and aft ends of the boat were decked, and these areas had oar-holes and rowing benches. Vessels of this sort did not have oars up their entire length and had a relatively short endurance due to the fatigue of their small crews.

Ship Terminology

As might be expected, terminology varies somewhat regarding Viking ships, and is sometimes misapplied or contradictory.

RIGHT: **A Viking merchant ship, with a small well in the deck for cargo (or in this case livestock). Merchant ships may have been more rounded than fighting longships, although designs varied and some vessels served as both.**

A seagoing ship, i.e. one designed to operate in open rather than coastal waters, was termed a *hafskip*, while one serving as a merchant ship was known as a *kaupskip*. The term *langskip*, or longship, was often applied to a vessel specifically designed for military purposes, but many references to 'longships' actually describe trading vessels termed *knorrs*, or other, similar vessels.

It is entirely likely that certain words were used to describe different kinds of ship in different places or times, and that the same vessel type might have been given a different name elsewhere. The words that we associate today with the various types of Viking ship are not the same as modern class designations. It is possible to describe a modern warship by its class and any variant designation, and to find only minor variations between examples; the converse is not true of craftsman-built vessels of the ancient world, where each example of a general type might be different to the others.

This did not matter much to a Viking mariner. He knew how many men or items of cargo his vessel could carry, he knew how fast it would go and how far he could sail on one load of supplies. He knew the ships of his friends, and those of his rivals by reputation, and he could predict the capabilities of an unknown ship to within a reasonable margin just by looking at it. He did not need to file precise specifications with a central shipping registry, and nor did he care much if his vessel was 46cm (18in) longer than the average for that 'class'. All he cared about was its seaworthiness, capacity, reliability and speed.

Many Viking ships were of extremely similar design and may have changed designation as they changed roles. A ship was essentially just a means of water transport and access to a shore. Its cargo might be furs and fish one journey, and bloodthirsty raiders the next. Of the vessels termed 'longships' and primarily used by the raiders, the *Snekkja* was most common. This was a narrow vessel capable of carrying about 40 men. Snekkja designs varied from place to place – those built by Danes tended to have shallower draught than Norwegian and Icelandic vessels, which operated in deep-water fjords and the open sea.

The *Skei* was a larger vessel, or more likely a term for several different larger longships. The largest Skei may have been capable of carrying as many as 80 men, but historical references tend to credit the larger longships, of which those referred to as Skei were one type, as carrying about 60. It is hard to determine exactly what vessels are being referred to sometimes as alternative terms are often used.

Dragon Ships
Many English and other sources refer to Viking longships as 'dragon ships' and speak of dragon-shaped carvings on the prow.

LEFT: The deceptively simple construction of Viking longships was so effective that it changed little for many decades. These vessels were constructed for coastal waters but managed to brave the North Atlantic swell.

Archaeologists have found examples with snakes and other monsters, but no dragons to date. However, a snake-headed ship is quite frightening enough when it is filled with Viking raiders, and a certain amount of mythology may have crept into accounts of the raids. In any case, references to 'dragon ships' do not give us the precise specifications or even class designations of the vessels involved.

Ship Designs

The design of longships and other seagoing vessels changed little during the Viking Age. Advanced and efficient vessels were available in 793 AD, and even three centuries later the Vikings were sailing the same waters to carry out the same missions. Their ships did not really need to change, so they did not.

Hulls were clinker-built, i.e. their construction used overlapping oak planks held together by iron nails. The sides of the vessel were linked by cross-beams, and light ribs supported the hull members. This gave the vessel a flexibility that allowed it to cope with the stresses caused by waves in open water. Removable planks were used to form a deck to walk on, which was slightly raised near the fore and aft ends of the ship.

Modern reconstructions have produced a vessel that could twist and flex up to 15cm (6in) in a swell, which must have been alarming to modern people used to metal vessels but was probably considered normal by the Vikings. Indeed, this flexibility gave the Viking longship a sense of being a live thing that slid through the sea rather than simply bashing its way through the waves. This flexing could open up holes in the hull, but clinker-built Viking ships were surprisingly watertight. This was in part assisted by the use of hair, wool or other materials soaked in pitch. During the winter the ships were brought ashore and their waterproofing renewed, with the vessel then left to dry until sailing conditions were acceptable once again.

The keel was a single piece of timber for most of its length, joining to curved pieces that formed the prow and sternposts. Large wooden blocks around the keel anchored the mast, which

'A PERSON SHOULD TRUST THEIR OWN EXPERIENCE RATHER THAN HEARSAY.'

became a little more sophisticated as time went on. The mast could be unstopped quickly at need, and served as a support for a tent covering the decks at night when the ship was hove-to and the sail taken down.

The large, square sail was supported on a single yard and was made of wool. The traditional image of Viking ships with striped red-and-white sails is borne out by archaeological finds; the red stripes were created by sewing coloured cloth to the sail. The sail was used whenever possible in open waters, but oars provided propulsion in combat and close to the shore, as well as in calm weather. The oars passed through holes in the third plank down from the gunwales, which had shutters on the inside to permit the ports to be closed. The oars themselves were of pine, and each one was custom made for its position on the ship. The differing lengths ensured that all the oars could be used in unison for an even stroke.

A Hard Life

Life aboard a longship was hard, with turns at the oars required whenever there was no favourable wind and constant exposure to the harsh sea environment. The tent, rigged at night, offered a little protection but for the most part the Vikings aboard went about their business in an open vessel. Nevertheless, they seem to have loved their ships and not only for the capabilities they brought. A ship was a status symbol and it gave the Viking owner the opportunity to raid or trade. It represented freedom and the ability to leave behind troubles at home for a time, or even to relocate to new lands.

More than that, it seems that the Vikings' ships were part of their cultural identity. They are referred to in dramatic terms by saga-poets, who often use figures of speech called *kennings* to describe people and objects. Ships are described as 'oar-steed' or 'surf-dragon' in the sagas, in terms of admiration and affection.

In addition to their crews, longships had to carry cargo and provisions plus the usual

BELOW: No surviving longship prow has been found in the shape of a dragon, suggesting that the term 'dragon ships' may not have originated with carved prows. Serpents have been found, however, which may have prompted the dragon label.

RIGHT: **A surviving Viking longship, possibly a knorr, which was sunk as a blockship in the Roskilde Fjord. This vessel would have had a cargo capacity around 24 tons, and dates from the late Viking Age, perhaps around 1030–1050 AD.**

paraphernalia of seagoing voyages – rope, anchors, spare timbers and the like. The practice of hanging shields on the outside of the boat probably stemmed from Viking pragmatism – it provided a handy place to carry the shields where they would not get in the way, and helped protect the oarsman from arrows in combat and from the weather the rest of the time. This protection was not needed when the oarsman left his bench to fight, so rather than carry the extra weight all the time, the shipbuilders made use of the Viking's shield in a way that also kept it handy for when he needed it.

This practice reflects the philosophy behind Viking shipbuilding in general – no space or weight is wasted and maximum use is made of every possible feature. Ships were double-ended to allow them to reverse quickly. This was useful when launching from a beach, possibly with recently raided locals in pursuit, but it also proved handy when operating in the narrow waters of the fjord. Rather than turn around in a confined area, the ship could simply exit by effectively swapping ends.

Modern Reconstructions

Modern reconstructions of Viking vessels have made impressive voyages, including a crossing in 1893 from Bergen in Norway to Newfoundland. The voyage was made in sometimes stormy conditions and took 28 days. This impressive feat taught the crew much about Viking seamanship and demonstrated the longship's remarkable ability to flex in heavy seas, but more importantly it proved that it was possible to cross the Atlantic in an open boat. To have reached the Americas from Greenland now seems not merely plausible but almost inevitable given the nature of the people involved.

These modern reconstructions have managed speeds of 10 or 11 knots (18–20km/h), which is very respectable for any vessel. Some sources credit the best Viking vessels with being even faster than this, although in most instances it was endurance and sustained speed that were the most important factors. An extra knot or two might help catch or outrun enemies but the ability to sail in open waters for a lengthy period at a good speed was more important over the course of an expedition.

Under oars, a top speed of about 4 knots (7km/h) has been demonstrated by reconstructions, but this is only sustainable for a few minutes. Two knots or perhaps a little more is a reasonable sustained speed, and this estimate is borne out by Viking records that give a rower's shift as 1000 strokes. A series of estimates and extrapolations places this as about two hours at the oars covering about 7.4km (four nautical miles), suggesting a sustained speed of 2 knots under normal conditions.

LEFT: A replica longship on the River Ouse in York. Experimental archaeology has revealed much about how the Vikings lived, and today there are many people who live the Viking life just for fun.

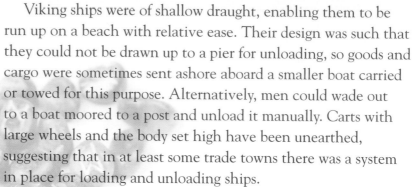

Viking ships were of shallow draught, enabling them to be run up on a beach with relative ease. Their design was such that they could not be drawn up to a pier for unloading, so goods and cargo were sometimes sent ashore aboard a smaller boat carried or towed for this purpose. Alternatively, men could wade out to a boat moored to a post and unload it manually. Carts with large wheels and the body set high have been unearthed, suggesting that in at least some trade towns there was a system in place for loading and unloading ships.

The shallow draught of Viking ships assisted in other ways. It was possible to land on islands or remote stretches of coast where deeper-draught vessels, such as those in use elsewhere, simply could not go. This allowed a crew or even a fleet to rest in a safe place, while anyone who wanted to fight them had either to wait offshore until they came out or sail around looking for a place to land and then move overland to attack. There was of course little to stop the Vikings from simply sailing away at this point.

The keel also served as a measure of depth, which was important during an attack or raid. The usual means of disembarkation was to leap or vault over the side, and it was rarely possible to see how deep the water was just by looking. A ship that had grounded its keel provided a measure of depth; the Viking warrior knew that he was jumping essentially from the

RIGHT: Getting ashore was a hazardous time for a raiding crew. Until enough men were ashore to defend the landing site the entire force was vulnerable to counterattack.

height of the ship's gunwales to the depth of the keel, and would be able to avoid leaping headlong into deep water. A gangplank was used by those in less of a hurry.

Overland Transport

Water transport was extremely important to the Vikings, who used small boats on rivers and fjords as well as ships on the sea. Overland travel on the local scale was not much of a problem – most routine journeys were short enough that walking sufficed. Carts were used if goods had to be transported, and these were pulled by oxen or possibly horses.

ABOVE: Skis were used for personal transport by Vikings living in snow-bound areas. The use of mismatched skis and a single pole left a hand free for other activities, although fighting on skis was probably a difficult skill to learn.

Sledges were a common mode of transport in colder areas, and skis and snowshoes were used to assist personal mobility in snowy conditions. Mismatched skis were used with a single pole; one ski was for gliding along and the other, which was shorter, was for propulsion. Ice skates are referred to in some sources as being used by traders to bring their goods over frozen rivers, but they were more commonly used for recreation and challenges of skill.

Warriors used horses for strategic mobility, while rich people used them as personal transport; iron spikes were sometimes fitted to the horse's hooves for grip on ice. Viking horses were not large, but they were hardy and capable of long journeys at a reasonable speed. Over short distances they were probably nothing like as fast as those later used by people such as the Normans, who rode into battle, but the small Viking horse was entirely acceptable as a mount for getting from place to place, especially for a warrior who expected to fight dismounted.

Saddles, including pack-saddles, have been excavated and seem to have been positioned well back on the horse, with the rider's feet pushed forward in his stirrups. The Normans adopted this system, probably in direct continuance from their Viking heritage. Vikings also used spurs and metal bridles, which were commonly of a snaffle type similar to those used today.

8

THE VIKING KINGDOMS

At the beginning of the Viking Age, the states and kingdoms were tiny by the standards of later societies but were capable of undertaking large works of construction. The *Danevirke*, a system of fortifications running right across Denmark, was constructed to defend the area from incursions by Germanic tribes to the south.

Although originally attributed to King Godfred, work on the Danevirke is now known to have begun in the 730s AD. The Danevirke was a major undertaking, requiring the coordination of a great deal of labour as well as all the planning, surveying and logistics tasks that go into building a great fortification. Its construction shows that the Vikings were capable of large-scale organization even before the dawn of the Viking Age. On a more modest scale, they were also capable of building good-quality seagoing ships for trade and raiding.

At this time, the Viking lands of Denmark, Sweden and Norway had a growing population, and it has been suggested

OPPOSITE: **Although they are primarily remembered as destructive raiders, the Vikings were also quite capable of building sophisticated defensive works, towns and tombs that have lasted, in some cases, to the present day.**

that the Viking Age was triggered by a need for more land. This may have been a factor but it cannot have been the only reason; Scandinavia was in no way overpopulated at this time. It has also been suggested that improvements in technology contributed to Viking expansion, notably an increase in the amount of iron that could be worked into tools and weapons.

In all probability the Viking expansion was a combination of many factors, not the least of which was the natural adventurism of the people themselves. They believed that the strong and hardy had a right to whatever they could take, and this was not just limited to property. Social status was gained the same way as wealth in many cases, and if a man found good land to settle, then it was natural and proper for him to take it and make it his own. The Viking expansion was, therefore, a natural progression from their society and social values, made possible by a strong economy, a good industrial base and sufficient population. Given these factors, it was perhaps inevitable that Vikings would settle over a wide area and ultimately come to dominate a huge expanse of Europe and beyond.

Vikings in Russia

There are differing schools of thought about the level of Viking influence in Russia. Some contend that the Vikings founded many of the major cities of modern Russia; others hotly refute this. What is known is that Viking settlements crept up the rivers around Lake Ladoga and Lake Onega, and the local Slavic peoples were subject to the usual raids while also benefiting from trade with the Vikings. Viking adventurers were able to force some Russian tribes into paying them tribute, but around 860 AD they were driven out. However, when the region collapsed into chaos they came back, according to some sources at the invitation of the locals. Scandinavia was at the time a land of petty-kingdoms, so it made perfect sense for Viking warriors to set up a similar system in Russia. Three kinsmen came to rule Novgorod, Beloozero and Izborsk. The only one to survive more than a year or two, and

'WITH MANY WHO COME TO POWER AND HONOR, PRIDE KEEPS PACE WITH PROMOTION.'

LEFT: Lake Ladoga was a natural path for Viking expansion, allowing them to move into Russia via the lake and its associated waterways. Expansion and settlement in this direction took place on a small scale even when there were no great expeditions underway.

take control of the region, was a man called Rurik. His followers were given cities to govern.

According to one version of the Russian Primary Chronicle, Rurik settled first near Lake Ladoga and founded the city of Ladoga, although there is archaeological evidence that there was already a settlement at that location when Rurik arrived. Similarly, Rurik and his followers are credited with founding Novgorod as their new capital, although there may well have already been a city or at least a settlement of some sort present when they arrived. Other histories vary, but the prevailing picture is that the Vikings created a military ruling class in the region under whose governance a number of cities grew up.

The Viking-led Slavs of this area became known as Rus, although there is a lot of debate about the origins of that word. Similarly, it is debatable whether the Vikings took control over a chaotic area and built a society, or simply moved in at the top of the existing social order. It has been suggested that rather

OPPOSITE: **Rivers and lakes permitted the movement of greater quantities of goods than would have been possible overland, making the long trip to Constantinople and back a lucrative, if hazardous, venture.**

than taking over, the Vikings were integrated and their influence was, in fact, smaller than often believed. Perhaps the most likely scenario is that the Vikings migrated into the region and found a niche for themselves. As fighting-men in a troubled time, this was close to the top of the social order and many Vikings joined the ruling class. If this was the case then there was no takeover as such, and no founding of a new state, but instead a change in both groups as they amalgamated into something new.

Whatever the truth may be, many of the people the Rus had contact with thought of them as Vikings, and referred to Vikings as Rus. They may not have been aware that there was a Viking homeland that was not in Russia, and simply assumed that anyone who looked and acted like a Rus was one.

BELOW: **By the 990s, the Rus firmly controlled Novgorod and Kiev. To many their Viking Slavic society was synonymous with Vikings everywhere, although there were cultural differences between Norwegian and Icelandic Vikings.**

The Kievan Rus

Rurik's descendants moved the Rus capital to Kiev, and the people of the region became known as the Kievan Rus. By this time, the two cultures were thoroughly intertwined and it is quite possible that some of the fortifications built by the Kievan Rus were actually constructed to keep more Vikings from coming in.

Experience gained in portaging ships down the Russian rivers came in handy when the Rus attacked Constantinople in 907 AD.

The Viking River Road
to Constantinople

→ Viking trade routes

Their fleet emerged from the Dnieper and crossed the Black Sea to attack the Byzantine capital. The defenders hoped that a boom of iron chains would prevent the Rus from entering the Bosporus, but this was simply another portage to the Vikings. With the Rus fleet around the chains and advancing on their capital, the Byzantines agreed to a treaty. This amounted largely to trade concessions, indicating the importance of trade to the Rus and other Viking societies. There was one intriguing clause, however – a requirement that the Rus should be able to take a bath as often as they liked when they were in Constantinople.

The Kievan Rus were at this time powerful enough to treat with the Byzantine Empire on favourable terms, and continued to be a major force in the region until just after the end of the Viking Age. However, somewhere along the way, the Rus had ceased to be Vikings as such and were now a Viking-influenced state with its own identity. This progression was repeated elsewhere over a similar time period.

The Scandinavian Kingdoms

The rise of a unified kingdom in Scandinavia can be traced – not surprisingly perhaps – to a rather bloody episode in which King Gudrod the Hunter raided the neighbouring kingdom of Agdir and carried off Asa, the king's daughter, to be his bride. Gudrod is a somewhat vague figure in historical reference, but his descendants are better known. His kingdom was probably located in Vestfold.

Gudrod was assassinated around 840 AD, at which point his wife returned home to Agdir with her young son Halfdan. His parentage gave him inheritance rights over Gudrod's kingdom, and around 860 AD he was able to claim half of it from his half-brother, Olaf Geirstada-Alf. This gave Halfdan a powerbase that he used to conquer other small kingdoms. Others were brought under his influence by bargaining from a position of power. Halfdan, known as Halfdan the Black, was a powerful man, but his was only one of the petty-kingdoms of Norway. His holdings lay on the coast but were separated by other lands.

It is possible that Asa, mother of Halfdan the Black, was buried at Oseberg. A large ship-burial was found there, which contained a female who was clearly of great wealth and importance. The age of the burial ties in with evidence from the sagas, and there is reason to suppose that this was the resting place of Queen Asa. If so, the richness of the burial, aboard a fine ship and surrounded by grave-goods, makes perfect sense, for Queen Asa was the grandmother of the first king of a unified Norway.

King Harald

Asa's son Halfdan died at the age of about 40, somewhere between 870 and 880 AD. He was drowned when his horse fell through ice on a frozen lake, leaving behind a son named Harald. According to legend, a seeress prophesied Harald's rise to power, although of course this account may have been a later embellishment. What is known is that Harald inherited his father's kingdom at the age of 10 or so, and was immediately challenged by other rulers who sought to take land from the boy king.

BELOW: The battle of Hafrsfjord was the largest battle in Norwegian history at the time, and is popularly considered to be the point where a unified kingdom was forged. Harald Fine-Hair's victory removed all serious opposition to his rule.

ABOVE: **The Swords in the Mountain sculpture was created in the early 1980s to commemorate the Battle of Hafrsfjord. The largest of the swords represents King Harald; the smaller ones are his enemies.**

Harald's realm survived, and he became very taken with a princess named Gyda from Hordaland. She rebuffed his advances, with rather unexpected consequences for world politics. Rather than resort to the tactics of his grandfather Gudrod and try to capture her, Harald instead swore not to cut or comb his hair until he had conquered all of Norway.

This was a huge undertaking, guaranteed to impress Harald's prospective bride and everyone else. It was also a very grave oath, as Vikings were supposed to take good care of their hair. Harald became known as Harald Mop-Hair during the next decade, and probably resembled the popular image of the wild-haired savage Viking as he made war upon those Norwegian kings who would not ally with him. Finally, as the first ruler of all of Norway, Harald won Gyda over, and had his hair cut for the first time in years. This must have improved his appearance, as henceforth he was known as Harald Fine-Hair.

Harald's conquest of Norway drove many Vikings overseas. Some left to avoid the consequences of having taken sides against him; others simply did not like the situation and set up home elsewhere. Some created bases and raided coastal trade, prompting a further campaign to suppress what amounted to pirate bases in the Scottish isles. Harald also had to deal with petty-kings and Jarls whose ships operated out of remote fjords.

Control of the sea trade up the Norwegian coast was politically and economically vital to Harald, and his opponents did not give up easily. A confederation of what were individually fairly minor chieftains posed the last great threat to Harald Fine-Hair's rule, until they were defeated in a pitched battle at Hafrsfjord near modern Stavanger. This probably took place around 890 AD, although traditionally the date has been given as 872 AD.

In addition to princess Gyda, Harald Fine-Hair had many concubines and several wives, and produced a large number of sons. The sagas are not always very reliable sources, as they were written from oral traditions centuries after the events they record, but in the case of Harald they speak of anything up to 20 sons. Twelve of these were named as kings, although in some cases they were granted a small petty-kingdom, and only two ruled over all of Harald's united Norway.

Harald Fine-Hair died around 933 AD, aged over 80. In his final years he co-ruled with his favourite son, Erik Bloodaxe, while his other offspring were granted lands that they used as a powerbase for their squabbles. Harald had sent his youngest son Haakon, to England, where he lived at the court of King Aethelstan. This was in keeping with the Viking tradition of fostering some children with other families, although in this case it had an important consequence. During his fosterage with Aethelstan, Haakon became a Christian.

> 'NEVER SWEAR FALSE OATHS; GREAT AND GRIM IS THE REWARD FOR THE BREAKING OF TROTH.'

Erik Bloodaxe

In the meantime, Erik Bloodaxe was foremost among Harald's sons. There is surprisingly little hard historical evidence about his life but the sagas have a lot to say about him. Apparently, Erik earned his name in the traditional Viking manner. He seems to have had a very successful career as a sea-raider, plundering his way around the Baltic and North Sea coasts, and even launched a raiding expedition down the River Dvina. He became king of Norway after his father's death and cemented his rule by thinning the ranks of his rivals. These included some or even several of his brothers and half-brothers. He rapidly made himself unpopular with the Jarls and the general population, ruling in the manner that earns a man a nickname like 'Bloodaxe'.

Eric's half-brother Haakon returned to Norway and was welcomed by Erik's opponents. Finding himself outmatched, Erik fled and, according to some sources, returned to a life of piracy and raiding. Eventually he landed in Northumberland, where he became king for a short time. During this period he came into renewed contact with Egil Skallagrimsson, hero of *Egil's Saga*. Egil had been outlawed by Eric while he was in Norway; the two had feuded and Egil had killed some of Eric's kin. Before leaving Norway, Egil had tried to set the land-spirits against Eric with a curse-pole, but the two were now reconciled.

Egil was shipwrecked, captured and brought before Eric Bloodaxe for judgement. Eric fully intended to have Egil put to death but was so impressed with a poem Egil had composed in his honour that instead he granted forgiveness and freedom to his old enemy. It is not known whether this incident actually happened or was an invention of saga-poets. In either case it serves to illustrate one aspect of the complex Viking character. 'Big deeds' were their way; Egil won over his sworn enemy with a heroic poem, while Erik's forgiveness of an enemy who had killed some of his kin was an equally grand gesture.

Egil went on his way, and Eric met his death in 954 AD at Stainmore. The circumstances are unclear but it seems that he was forced from his throne in Northumberland and killed in a rearguard action against his pursuers.

BELOW: One of the two great rune stones at Jelling was erected by Harald Bluetooth to commemorate his conquest of Denmark and Norway. It features a depiction of Christ and one of the earliest uses of the name Denmark.

From Greycloak to Knut

Meanwhile, Haakon had earned himself the nickname 'The Good' but constantly had to fight off challenges from Eric's sons. He was successful but was mortally wounded in 961 AD during a surprise attack on his royal residence at Fitjar. Haakon was generally successful during his reign, but in one area he failed utterly. He tried to convert his new subjects to Christianity, but failed to the extent that, upon his death, a heroic poem was composed in his honour. It spoke of his reception into Valhol even though he was a Christian.

After Haakon's death, Harald Greycloak, son of Erik Bloodaxe, became king over a greatly diminished realm.

He enjoyed the support of Harald Bluetooth of Denmark, at least at first. Harald Greycloak went on to defeat a number of rivals and regained control over the vital coastal trade route. As his power increased his reliance on Harald Bluetooth diminished, which displeased the Danish king. Harald Bluetooth transferred his support to Haakon Sigurdsson, Jarl of Lade. Haakon wanted vengeance for his father's death at the hands of Greycloak's troops, and he had him assassinated. Haakon became king of Norway as a vassal to Harald Bluetooth.

Harald Bluetooth had an eventful reign, which began in 958 AD with the death of his father, Gorm the Old. Even before this he was involved in foreign adventures, including a foray into Normandy. He converted to Christianity in the 960s AD, becoming the first Christian Viking king. After Harald Greycloak of Norway was assassinated, Harald Bluetooth received the allegiance of his successor, Haakon. He was thus, for a time, king of both Denmark and Norway.

Harald Bluetooth is sometimes credited with the construction of the Danevirke, but in all probability he merely added to it. The defensive structure was intended to keep invaders out of Denmark, but in 974 AD Harald's army was defeated there by Germanic warriors. The region was regained nine years later but Harald's power was greatly weakened. He lost control over Norway after 974 AD, and in 985 or 986 AD he was deposed by his son Svein Forkbeard.

Svein Forkbeard renewed his father's alliance with the Jarl of Lade, at this point Haakon's son Eric. This gave Svein control over much of Norway from 1000 AD onwards. He also campaigned against England from 1002 AD onwards. Svein's

ABOVE: **A depiction of the arrival of Svein Forkbeard in England, containing many anachronisms. The military equipment and ships depicted are medieval in appearance.**

attacks on England were for the most part financially motivated. He needed cash, and the traditional Viking way to get it was to attack someone. The English decided to buy off Svein with Danegeld (bribery), greatly enriching him.

Despite the bribes, or perhaps because they allowed him to outfit a proper invasion force, Svein launched a renewed attack on England in 1013 AD. He was able to drive King Aethelred into exile and took control over the country, but mere weeks after being crowned King of England on Christmas Day 1013 AD, Svein Forkbeard died. Svein's son Harald took the Danish crown, while his younger son Knut became King of England. Harald ruled as Harald II for four years and was succeeded by his brother Knut.

ABOVE: Knut inherited the throne of England from his father Svein, who lived just long enough to make himself king after a successful invasion paid for by bribes previously extorted from the English.

OPPOSITE: The Vikings were for a time major players in the affairs of Ireland, but they were often distracted by events elsewhere in the British Isles and never rose to complete dominance.

Ireland and the West

The gradual move westwards was definitely in progress by the 830s, and probably began earlier. Viking settlers landed in the Scottish isles and set up homes there, progressing around the coast of Scotland to colonize the Hebrides and then on to Ireland, where the first Viking settlements were probably intended to be temporary, but over time grew into fortified towns from which raiding and trade expeditions could be launched. Among these towns was Dublin, founded in 840 or 841 AD. Dublin served as a base for Viking attempts at expansion not just in Ireland but also in Scotland and England.

A number of Viking chieftains styled themselves as kings in Dublin, with varying degrees of power and prestige. The Irish repeatedly attempted to dislodge the Norsemen from their land, and although they at times had some success the Vikings retained a presence. A wave of settlers arriving in the early 900s AD increased Viking power and allowed several towns to be founded, including Limerick and Waterford. However, the situation in Ireland was part of a wider picture, and events or opportunities elsewhere in the British Isles frequently distracted the Vikings and prevented consolidation of their position.

In 997 AD, for example, King Sigtrygg Silk-Beard established a mint in Dublin, but the coinage was mainly used for trade outside Ireland. Trade missions sailed all the way to Scandinavia or around the coast to trade with the Viking kingdom centred on York. This may have been due to ongoing conflict with the Irish; in 980 AD, the Vikings had suffered a serious defeat at the Battle

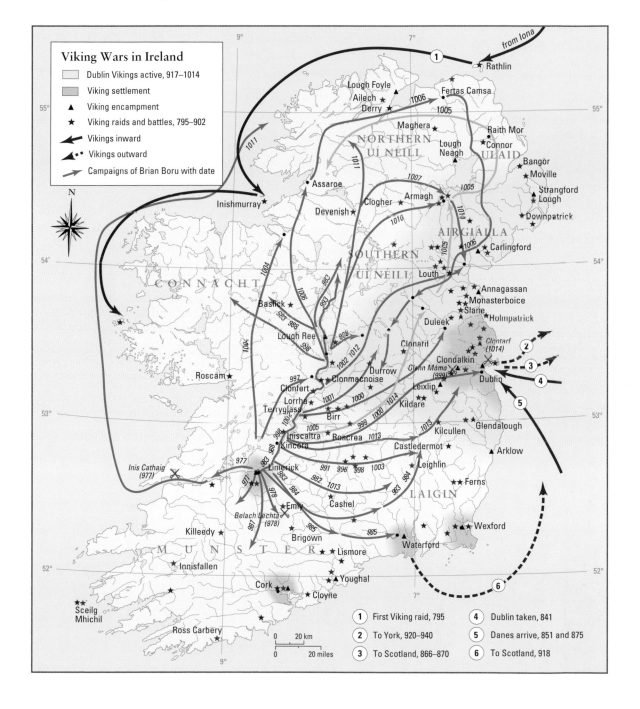

Viking Wars in Ireland

- Dublin Vikings active, 917–1014
- Viking settlement
- ▲ Viking encampment
- ★ Viking raids and battles, 795–902
- ◀ Vikings inward
- ◀•• Vikings outward
- Campaigns of Brian Boru with date

① First Viking raid, 795
② To York, 920–940
③ To Scotland, 866–870
④ Dublin taken, 841
⑤ Danes arrive, 851 and 875
⑥ To Scotland, 918

0 — 20 km
0 — 20 miles

of Tara, and their power had been declining for a long time. By 1014 AD, the Vikings were a relatively minor factor in Irish affairs and their stronghold at Dublin was under threat. Brian Boru, determined to become high king of the Irish, wanted the city for his capital. His forces engaged an alliance of Vikings from Ireland and elsewhere, fighting alongside the King of Leinster who was in revolt against Brian Boru. The Leinster/Viking alliance was decisively defeated although King Brian was killed. There was no real attempt to dislodge the remaining Vikings from Ireland afterwards, but the Vikings were reduced to the level of minor players in a very complex political situation.

The situation was very different in Iceland, where the Vikings were able to settle unopposed. The first settlers arrived in the 870s AD and within 50 years Iceland had become another Viking homeland. Many of those who settled there did so to escape from the conflict in Scandinavia at that time or pursuit by King Harald Fine-Hair. Many of Harald's enemies had fled to the Scottish islands when he became king in Norway, but decided to relocate farther away when he came after them. Iceland was at the time as far as a Viking could get from Norway, and so became the new home of these émigrés.

Democracy in Iceland

Although petty-kingdoms were the norm in Viking society, and a unified kingdom was emerging in Norway, the Icelanders were not keen on the idea and instead implemented a workable representative democracy. Power was vested in the Godi, priest-chieftains whose influence depended on the support of the general populace, and it came to be said of the Icelanders that 'they have no king but the law'. Perhaps this was in part a reaction to Harald's rise to power in Norway.

BELOW: Despite the death of Irish king Brian Boru at the battle of Clontarf in 1014 AD, his Viking opponents' power was broken. Although the Vikings retained a presence in Ireland they ceased to have much importance.

The key to the process of government in Iceland was the *Althing*, the annual meeting of Godi from all parts of the country at which any man could be heard and his points discussed by those in attendance. At the Althing, the Godi and their advisors made law and ruled on legal matters. The Althing was established in 930 AD and marked the emergence of Iceland as a nation in its own right rather than a collection of settlers from various Viking homelands.

Christianity was adopted in Iceland from 1000 AD onwards, generally without much fanfare or conflict. At first the Vikings may have viewed the Christian god as just one more to add to their pantheon, but gradually the Christian faith displaced the Old Norse religion. The first Christian diocese was established in 1056 AD, but it was half a century before a second emerged. By then, the Viking Age was over and Iceland charted its own path into the future.

Expedition to Disaster

From Iceland, explorers sailed west and sighted the landmass later named Greenland. The name was given to attract settlers, but it was not entirely misleading. Settlement occurred during what is now known as the Medieval Warm Period, but even then only small areas of Greenland were habitable. Within the shelter of the southern fjords it was possible to raise crops and cattle, although the growing season was short and life was hard.

Greenland may have been known from about 900 AD, when an Icelandic mariner was blown far off course and ended up off the coast of an unknown land now known to be Greenland. The official date for the discovery of Greenland is around 980 AD, when Erik the Red explored the area. However, there are records of an expedition to settle there in 978 AD. This may have been sparked by a famine in Iceland, but whatever its inspiration the expedition ended in total disaster.

The colonists landed on the east coast of Greenland, which was uninhabitable, and were prevented from sailing home by bad weather. Disputes during the harsh winter they spent there resulted in fights and many deaths. As a result, the colonization of Greenland did not begin properly until 984 AD.

ABOVE: **Christianity at first existed alongside the old Norse religion, but eventually displaced it. The devout replaced Thor's hammer with a crucifix, although many were quite happy to display both.**

ABOVE: Greenland was discovered by mariners blown off course by storms. They found a forbidding and harsh land that could nevertheless support a colony of tough settlers.

The voyage to the new land was arduous and conditions were harsh even by the standards of Iceland. Only 14 of the initial 25 ships actually reached their destination. Over time, however, the population grew to a peak of about 3000–5000 people. The Greenlanders were sufficiently remote to be a tiny nation in their own right; it was difficult for outsiders to interfere in their affairs, even if there was a reason to do so.

Changes in the climate caused the area to become less habitable, and by the 1300s it was virtually impossible to survive there. Drift ice made sea trade dangerous, and the Greenlanders had little to trade with anyway. Many moved away, to Newfoundland among other places. Those who remained gradually died out due to malnourishment.

But long before this tragic end overtook them, the Greenland Vikings reached the Americas and even settled there. Centuries before European explorers 'discovered' America, Vikings were living in Canada, albeit on a small scale.

Voyage to the Americas

The discovery of the Americas took place in 986 AD, just a few years after Greenland was sighted, but it was 15 years before Leif

Eriksson undertook his voyage of exploration. Exactly where he explored and landed is open to some debate. There are references to three areas explored by his ships. The first was named Helluland, or 'Slab Land'. This disparaging name suggests that the Vikings were not impressed with this first landfall, which was probably on Baffin Island.

Helluland became a stopover point on voyages from Greenland to their settlements in the New World, and it is likely that the Vikings traded with the locals on some of their later voyages. A carved wooden doll found in the 1970s is executed in the classic Eskimo style, but depicts a man wearing a long Viking-like cloak and an amulet with cross on it. It seems to be a depiction of a Christian Viking seafarer, and lends credence to various saga references to expeditions landing on Helluland. However, it appears that no locals were met on the first visit.

Unimpressed with Baffin Island, Leif Eriksson sailed onwards and landed on what we now know to be the coast of Labrador. This was rather better, with white sandy beaches that later visitors would term *Furdustrandir*, or 'Wonder Strands'. Leif considered the region's forests to be its main feature and named this land Markland, or 'Forest-Land'.

Departing Markland, the expedition sailed on and found an island where they went ashore before navigating a river into the interior of the nearby mainland. A brief exploration showed that this place was ideal for settlement. There were plenty of fish in the rivers and the grass grew more abundantly than in Greenland. The discovery that there were grapes growing nearby was an added bonus, but was probably not why Leif named this place Vinland. The name has been interpreted as meaning 'land of vines' but a better translation would be 'meadows'.

In 1001 AD Leif's expedition spent the winter in the New World. They were probably

BELOW: **The sagas include an account of Viking explorers finding grapes growing wild, leading to the new land being named Vinland. Other explanations for the name have also been put forward.**

on the north coast of Newfoundland, although it has been suggested that they landed further south. The Vikings explored for as long as they were able, then returned to Greenland. Their camp was reused by the next expedition, under Leif's brother Thorvald. This group also wintered in Newfoundland where they came into conflict with the local inhabitants.

Conflict and Trade

The Vikings knew of people living in the New World. They had found evidence in Greenland of boats and tools – primitive compared to theirs but entirely capable of supporting people living in the harsh local conditions. The Vikings named these people Skraelings, meaning 'wretches', and managed to get into a fight with the first band they encountered. Most of the locals were killed but the survivors came back with reinforcements and an attack on the camp ensued. Although the Vikings had prudently fortified their camp (most likely a precaution against the weather and possible attack), Thorvald was killed by an arrow. Another brief expedition followed, this time led by another of Leif's brothers, Thorstein.

'WHO CAN SAY WHAT SORROW SEEMINGLY CAREFREE FOLK BEAR TO THEIR LIFE'S END.'

Although the exploration of the new land had shown the natives to be unfriendly (or, at least, not receptive to being attacked by Vikings), Vinland offered a number of possibilities. Not least was the prestige and word-fame to be earned from being First Settler there. On top of that the new country offered good farming land and a chance to carve out a territory as large as a man dared to claim. The new land also had timber, which was in short supply in Greenland.

In 1009 or 1010 AD Thorfinn Karlsefni led an expedition to colonize Vinland. Thorfinn was now a member of the Eriksson family, having married Erik the Red's daughter-in-law Gudrid while wintering in Greenland. Thorfinn was an Icelandic merchant, and like all good Vikings he was willing to take advantage of opportunities. Leif Eriksson, however, was determined to retain his position as First Settler in Vinland, and leased rather than sold Thorfinn the rights to make use of his

camp in Vinland. Thorfinn landed there with three ships, 60 men and five women, including his new bride. During their three-year stay Thorfinn and Gudrid had a son, Snorri. Snorri Thorfinnsson was, if the saga accounts are to be believed, the first child of European stock to be born in the Americas.

The Viking colonists traded with the locals, whom they still called Skraelings and apparently viewed with just as much contempt as previously. The Vikings apparently cheated the locals in trade, coming away with foodstuffs and valuable furs. The Skraelings attacked Thorfinn's settlement, which was protected by a stockade, and at first the Vikings held out.

One advantage the Vikings possessed was their military technology. Equipped with the very latest designs of European steel weaponry and body armour, they proved a match for the

ABOVE: Despite superior arms and equipment the Viking settlers could not withstand the ferocity of the Native Americans, and they withdrew their colony. This had grave implications for the settlers in Greenland.

RIGHT: **The Viking colony at L'Anse aux Meadows has been positively identified, and is today the site of a reconstructed Viking settlement.**

Skraelings' superior numbers. However, the locals, despite being far behind in the arms race due to their stone-age weaponry, were cunning and determined. They made life impossible for the Viking settlers who left after three years. This established the Native American population as one of the few peoples ever to have sent the Vikings packing, albeit on a small scale.

The Viking settlement in the Americas was withdrawn in 1015 AD, although it is possible that trade expeditions from Iceland and other Viking homelands continued to cross the Atlantic for several hundred years. This had almost certainly ceased by the time Europeans celebrated the discovery of the New World, which explains why they did not run into anyone who could greet them in a Norwegian dialect.

The location of the Viking settlement in Newfoundland is open to some debate. There is some speculation that the Vikings might have explored farther south down the coast, or settled at a different location. However, it is known that they did build homes on Newfoundland. In the 1960s a site was discovered and excavated at L'Anse aux Meadows at the northern tip of Newfoundland. Artefacts from the site are of Viking origin and date from around 1000 AD.

It is still not certain that L'Anse aux Meadows is the site of Leif Eriksson's camp and the later Vinland colony, but it seems likely. The original 'land of vines' translation of Vinland suggested a site farther south, as vines do not grow so far north, but 'land of meadows' describes Newfoundland well enough and the saga references to landing on a peninsula reinforce this theory.

Whether or not L'Anse aux Meadows is the actual site of the main Viking colony, or one of several small settlements set up at the same time, is still open to some speculation. It is definitely a place where Vikings made their home, and from it they undoubtedly explored the surrounding area. Other finds of Viking items in North America are questionable at best and in most cases have been dismissed as hoaxes.

Of course, the Vikings traded with the locals when they were not fighting them, and a few Viking artefacts could have found their way deep into the interior without any Vikings ever seeing that land. On the other hand, the interior of the mainland is penetrated by several major rivers of which the nearest is the St Lawrence. Given the propensity of Viking mariners to sail up rivers on the lookout for opportunities, it is not impossible that parties of explorers did indeed penetrate the interior of the Americas, at least for a short time.

Britain and Northern Europe

Vikings had almost certainly visited the British Isles before the incident in 789 AD and the infamous Lindisfarne raid of a few years later. Settlement of the Shetland and Orkney islands began soon after this date, and by 865 AD the Great Army had landed in Britain. This was not a raid but a large-scale campaign of conquest, which led to the formation of a Viking kingdom centred on York. The city was named Jorvik in Danish, a corruption of its Old English name of Eoforwic.

In the mid 870s AD, Halfdan of the Wide Embrace and his brother Guthorm divided the Great Army and also, it seems, the Viking lands in England. Halfdan led his force, composed mostly of men from the original contingent of the Great Army, into Northumbria. They built

BELOW: During the 1960s, Anne Stine Ingstad and her husband Helge Ingstad conducted the excavations that proved L'Anse Aux Meadows to be a Viking site.

ANNE STINE og HELGE INGSTAD

De oppdaget vikingenes Amerika

a camp on the Tyne and from there launched an expedition into Strathclyde, attempting to conquer the Pictish kingdoms.

Halfdan's endeavour was launched in conjunction with Irish Vikings from the kingdom of Dublin; relations between Viking Northumbria and Dublin were good and the two kingdoms were closely associated until the demise of Dublin as a major Viking centre. However, this expedition ended in failure and most of Halfdan's men wanted an end to warfare.

Tired of tramping up and down England fighting all comers, much of Halfdan's contingent of the Great Army settled in York and the surrounding area. Some formed a well-armed social elite; others were content to have some land to build a farmstead. Halfdan was satisfied with neither and was eventually killed in 877 AD during a skirmish at sea. He was, at the time, attempting to reassert Viking control over Dublin.

At around the same time that Halfdan and a small portion of the former Great Army were trying to conquer Ireland, and the remainder were settling down in Northumbria, Halfdan's brother Guthorm was launching a renewed attempt to conquer Wessex with his half of the Great Army. This was mainly composed of men who had arrived to reinforce the original contingent, and who were still hungry for land and plunder.

Although the Great Army was defeated in 878 AD by Anglo-Saxon King Alfred the Great, it had by this time wrought massive changes in the political landscape. The Vikings had conquered Northumbria, Mercia and East Anglia, all of which were sizable kingdoms for the time, and established major Viking kingdoms outside Scandinavia.

The peace treaty between Alfred and Guthorm, leader of the Great Army, established the Viking and Anglo-Saxon spheres of influence in England. The area under Viking rule became known as the Danelaw. If Guthorm had failed to take control of all England, he had at least ensured that the Viking takeover, within what was now the Danelaw, was accepted by other rulers and thus not subjected to constant challenge.

BELOW: Jorvik was a major centre for political and economic power, with trade coming in by sea from Europe, Scandinavia and beyond. Minted coinage of reliable value helped facilitate this high volume of commerce.

Guthorm became a Christian under the terms of the treaty, and Alfred adopted him as a son. Relations between Guthorm's kingdom in East Anglia and Alfred's in Wessex remained relatively peaceful throughout Guthorm's reign, which ended upon his death in 890 AD.

Jorvik

Further north, additional settlers arrived in what was now the Viking kingdom of Jorvik (York), an important political and economic centre since before the kingdom of Northumbria existed; it was logical that once control passed to the Vikings, York would be the capital. The site had appealed to the Romans and the Anglians, who ruled there before the Vikings. It was easily defended and well placed as a communications centre.

The Jorvik Vikings benefited from their predecessors' works: the Romans had fortified the city and the Anglians had maintained its defences. Viking-era works were added to these defences or replaced areas that had fallen into disrepair. Similarly, the Roman fortress at York, located on the site of York Minster, had remained in use by the Anglians. They probably used it as an administrative centre and it is likely that the Vikings did too.

ABOVE: **The landing of the Great Army in England was no raid, not even a raid in force. It was nothing less than an invasion, and ultimately it changed the course of English history.**

'THE BRAVE MAN WELL SHALL FIGHT AND WIN, THOUGH DULL HIS BLADE MAY BE.'

Under Viking rule York prospered more than ever before, doubling in population to around 30,000. The River Ouse gave it access to the North Sea and then to the rest of Europe. Soon, York was one of the most important economic centres in Europe and it became a gateway to Britain for trade from Scandinavia. The Viking influence on York can be seen today in street names ending in 'gate' (from *gaeta*, or road) and the general layout of the city. Later buildings followed the same pattern of streets, which is visible to this day.

The kingdom of Jorvik did not encompass all of Northumbria, but it was large enough to be very powerful. Over time, inevitably, it changed from being a new Viking homeland to a melding of Viking and Anglian cultures, a power in its own right on the political stage of Europe. Change was inevitable wherever the Vikings visited or settled, and it was a two-way street. When the Vikings took control of York and the surrounding area, most of the established population continued to do what they always had, and the local girls tended to like the clean, well-dressed and generally affluent Viking men more than their unwashed Anglian rivals.

Mixture of Cultures

The same pattern was repeated all over the Viking world; where they settled, cultures melded. In Russia, Viking houses were built by Slav craftsmen in the local style, creating some confusion about how much impact the Vikings actually had – it is possible to conclude from the fact that there are relatively few 'true' Viking artefacts, or obviously Viking-built structures, that they were not present in very great numbers, but this impression is misleading.

The same applies in England; in Jorvik, Vikings paid local craftsmen to erect dwellings and to carve art for them. Their art reflects the influence of Vikings working in the same trade or those who asked them to carve specific images. Sometimes, these were rendered in a way that blended Viking and Anglian styles, or preconceptions of what the client wanted and the craftsman understood. The art, structures and everyday items produced in the Viking kingdom of Jorvik evolved into a distinctly Anglo-Viking style, just as the kingdom itself ceased to be an offshoot of Scandinavia and became an independent power.

Political Change

The presence of strong Viking kingdoms on the eastern coast of England may have served to deter raiding from Scandinavia, but if so, then it was the power of these kingdoms that did so, and not the fact that they were ruled by distant kinsmen of the Scandinavian Vikings. The latter had been quite happy to raid, pillage and murder one another over trivial slights for all of their history; it is rather unlikely that raiding would be curtailed simply because some other Vikings had taken up residence in the region.

Raiding was less prevalent at this time, partly due to political changes. The *jarldoms* and petty-kingdoms were merging into large states for which warfare and raiding were tools of policy. The existence of states to which Danegeld could be paid offered the victims of Viking raids some chance of respite, provided the kingdom receiving the Danegeld was able to keep its people under control. Danegeld enriched the kingdom and translated to greater power, so there was a cycle of increasing strength and control.

BELOW: **Aldwych on the Thames was one of several Anglo-Saxon settlements in the region of what had been Roman Londinium. It was a natural landing point for the Vikings, as the Thames gave direct access to the North Sea.**

Raiding was reduced by politics, but also by the ability of the victims to fight back. Vikings did not raid merely as something to do on a wet afternoon, there were sound reasons for launching an attack. These included winning fame, taking plunder or seeking vengeance for a slight or injury. The latter case was a compelling reason – essentially, peer pressure might force raids to be launched against targets that were well defended or would yield little loot. But in the other cases, attacking a hard target or getting yourself outlawed for raiding an exempted area was unattractive.

Raids in Europe

There was at the time a great deal of Viking activity in Europe. Enclaves had existed there for some years, initially as raiding bases. From one such base, possibly on the Loire, Bjorn Ironside and another Viking leader named Hastein ventured into the Mediterranean Sea. It is possible that these men were sons of Ragnar Lodbrok, and if so his family must rank among the most influential people in human history.

Whatever their parentage, Bjorn and Hastein were successful Viking leaders who had sacked Paris in 857 AD. From there,

BELOW: A depiction of the Viking attack on Paris in 885 AD. The Vikings made use of siege engines and sophisticated techniques, including mining under the walls.

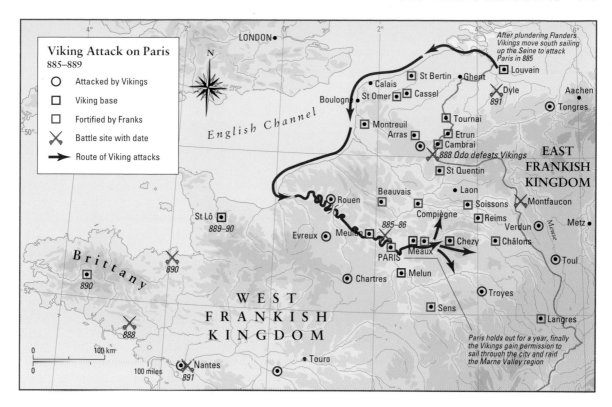

Viking Attack on Paris
885–889
○ Attacked by Vikings
□ Viking base
□ Fortified by Franks
✕ Battle site with date
➝ Route of Viking attacks

After plundering Flanders Vikings move south sailing up the Seine to attack Paris in 885

Paris holds out for a year, finally the Vikings gain permission to sail through the city and raid the Marne Valley region

they took with them a fleet of more than 60 ships and sailed around the coast into the Mediterranean on a lengthy plundering expedition. About a third of these ships survived; the fleet suffered defeats as well as successes along the way.

Despite setbacks, Bjorn and Hastein were able to sack towns and cities on the European and African shores of the Mediterranean, and also in the Balearic islands. According to some sources the fleet made a daring attack on an Italian city that they thought was Rome, pretending that their dying chieftain wanted to convert to Christianity and be buried in Christian style. Accounts of the 'corpse' leaping from his stretcher and the funeral party producing weapons from under their solemn robes certainly fits with the general image of Vikings as resourceful, cunning and having no regard for anyone's religion, including their own. However, the story is of questionable veracity.

According to legend, the Vikings plundered Luna and put most of the population to the sword to vent their annoyance when they realized that it was not Rome they were attacking. Modern archaeology has not uncovered evidence of this savage

ABOVE: **Larger forces enabled the Vikings to push deeper inland, but rivers were still their primary means of access. Fortresses on the rivers impeded their progress but could not completely deter their attacks.**

ABOVE: **Charles II's nickname 'the bald' may have been ironic, since he is recorded as having a lot of hair. He used the idea of Danegeld cleverly, bribing the Vikings to do something that suited his ends rather than simply paying them to not attack his holdings.**

sack, and the city as depicted did not exist in 860 AD. There was a city on that location but it was in decline and could not possibly have been mistaken for Rome.

Bjorn and Hastein's expedition was not the first into the Mediterranean; Seville was unsuccessfully attacked in 844 AD. However, it was a voyage that would win great word-fame (whether or not Luna was actually sacked) and guaranteed Hastein and Bjorn Ironside a place in history. Some sources claim that the fleet voyaged as far as Alexandria in Egypt before turning back to fight through the Moorish-held Straits of Gibraltar and return to the Loire.

Back in Europe, Hastein was involved in a series of military campaigns, sometimes alongside European forces such as those of Salomon of Brittany and sometimes independently. The Vikings were, by this time, a part of the European power structure and alliances with them were sought just like any other powerful state or group. At the same time, that power structure was disintegrating. The traditional power of the Church was declining, largely due to Viking attacks on its holdings. Towns and cities were building defences that could protect them against threats other than Viking raids; a well-defended town could perhaps defy its traditional overlords, and so new bargains were being struck. The Vikings were part of this demolition of the old order rather than being its sole instigators but they certainly rocked the boat a lot more than most other factions.

In 885 AD, the Vikings decided to sack Paris again. Some cities had been looted several times but Paris had been safe for a few years. That equated to a chance of renewed prosperity, and thus translated directly to plunder. Up to 700 Viking ships took part in the attack that was, all the same, unsuccessful in immediately storming the city. A siege developed and Paris took on the form of a roadblock to Viking progress deeper into France.

King Charles II of West Francia, sometimes called Charles the Bald, assembled a powerful army and threw a cordon around the Viking siege lines, recalling Roman tactics as he laid siege to the besiegers. Having made it clear that the Vikings were now in a bad position he offered them a bribe to leave. The Viking force was probably only too glad to accept money in order to remove itself from such a predicament. They also accepted an invitation to winter in Burgundy. Not coincidentally, Charles II was concerned about a rebellion in Burgundy. The Vikings were not only prevented from sacking Paris and northern France, they were turned into a useful instrument of policy.

England Invaded

Hastein was part of the Viking invasion of England in 892 or 893 AD, by which time he was one of the most important of all Viking war leaders. The force assembled for the invasion was large but the age when Vikings could pillage at will had passed. By the 890s AD, Europe was going through a period of what can be described as target-hardening. In the south of England, King Alfred the Great successfully defended his coasts with a fleet and his towns with a sophisticated and effective military system. His reign was hard, with many crises, and shortly before his death in 899 AD he faced this renewed Viking invasion.

Like the Great Army before it, this was no band of plunderers; it was an organized military force. The new invasion came across the English Channel, a Viking army that had gained experience marauding around Europe. In 892 AD, the invaders assembled at Boulogne and sailed across the Channel in two fleets. One sailed up the Thames, the other landed on the south coast of Kent. The intentions of this force were probably a combination of conquest and plundering; some of the Vikings would want to settle in good land, others were happy to strip it of valuables. It is also possible that the intent was to do some damage and take some plunder, then accept a bribe to withdraw from towns and cities that the host had captured – extortion on an industrial scale.

BELOW: This depiction of Rollo is typical of the way later images of Vikings reflected the armour and equipment of the time. In reality his arms and armour would have been more traditionally 'Viking' in appearance.

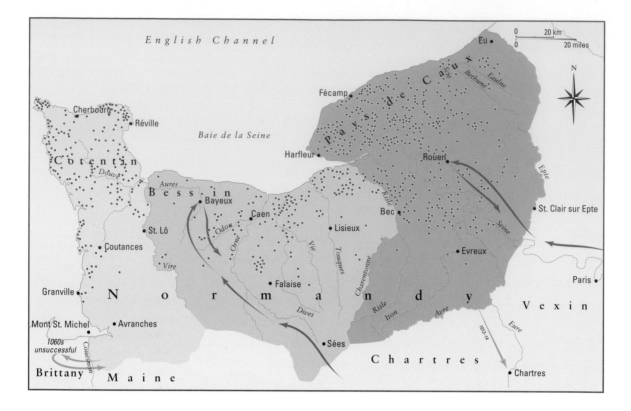

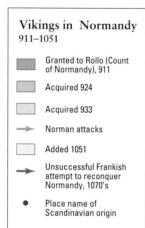

Vikings in Normandy
911–1051

Granted to Rollo (Count of Normandy), 911

Acquired 924

Acquired 933

→ Norman attacks

Added 1051

Unsuccessful Frankish attempt to reconquer Normandy, 1070's

● Place name of Scandinavian origin

Whatever the motives of the invaders, their plans went awry. The men of Wessex had been fighting Vikings for some time and had evolved an effective system for limiting their movements and bringing a powerful force to bear. Both forces were intercepted and defeated in battle. The Vikings retired to a defensible spot, perhaps hoping to extort Danegeld in return for withdrawing. This time a negotiated retreat was not acceptable, and they were driven from one location to another. The Vikings were not defeated each time they tried to stand and fight, but their force was worn down until, by 896 AD, the invasion had been defeated.

From Bandits to Kingdom-Builders

Some of the survivors joined the local Viking kingdoms but many went back across the Channel into Europe. Of them, some sought new opportunities with Rollo, a Viking leader whose origins are the source of some debate. He has been associated with the saga-hero Hrolf, who was so big that no horse could carry him. If so, he was outlawed in Norway and came to Francia by way of the Orkney Islands. He may have been among the men of the Great

THE VIKING KINGDOMS   199

Army that campaigned in England. Whatever his origins Hrolf, or Rollo, led a force that was defeated at Chartres in 911 AD. King Charles III of West Francia, sometimes called Charles the Fat, decided to follow in his father's footsteps and use the Vikings rather than fight them. In a less-than-solemn ceremony that has already been described, Charles III granted Rollo the lands his men were already occupying, making him Duke of Normandy.

In the short term, this was one of the most effective pieces of target-hardening possible; Charles III emplaced a horde of Vikings in the path of any new invasion. Over a longer period, events were set in motion that would bring the Viking Age to an end. Rollo's investiture as Duke of Normandy in many ways marked the end of the raiding age – raids would continue, but the situation had changed: the Vikings had become kingdom-builders.

This did not mean that voyages of exploration and plunder were not ongoing. As Rollo accepted land in Normandy, and the Viking kings consolidated their positions in Jorvik and East Anglia, Harald Fine-Hair was king in Norway and his opponents were settling in Iceland and the Scottish islands to escape his control. The settlement of Greenland was 70 years in the future.

These events were all intertwined to a greater or lesser degree. For a time, Erik Bloodaxe, deposed son of Harald Fine-Hair of Norway, would rule the Kingdom of Jorvik. Harald Hardrada, the last Viking king, would serve in the Varangian Guard, whose formation resulted, in part, from the demonstration of Viking fighting power in attacks on Constantinople.

Viking influence on the Mediterranean was small compared to other areas. Large-scale raids were mounted in the 960s, and small expeditions made the occasional foray, but there was nothing like the disruption in northern Europe. Nevertheless, ambassadors from Arab states sometimes journeyed to Scandinavia to conduct diplomacy at the Viking courts. Arabic coin reached Scandinavia mainly via Russia rather than the Mediterranean, and the Vikings remained, mostly, a distant rumour to the people of the Mediterranean.

OPPOSITE: The creation of a Viking kingdom in Normandy was a political masterstroke, but it also marks the transition from opportunistic raiders to kingdom-builders.

'A PERSON SHOULD NOT AGREE TODAY TO WHAT THEY'LL REGRET TOMORROW.'

9

THE END OF THE VIKING AGE

The year 1066 AD provides a clear date at which to end the Viking Age, but in truth it ended in various places at different times. In the Vinland colony the Vikings left in 1015 AD. In Greenland they struggled on until after the Viking Age was 'officially' over, although by then they were not really Vikings any more, but Greenlanders.

Similarly, the other Viking societies continued to evolve and become something quite different from their original society. The rise of unified kingdoms and the coming of Christianity saw the decline of the traditional raid-and-trade Viking methods, and cultural mingling resulted in 'Viking Kingdoms' that were in truth more like Anglo-Viking or Rus-Viking societies. This was perhaps inevitable; change is the only constant in the universe.

By the end of the Viking Age the fates of the Viking states around the North Sea were bound together. Iceland, Greenland and Russia were distant geographically and historically, but Scandinavia, northern Europe and Britain were linked by a web

OPPOSITE: William of Normandy was a Viking successor whose society had moved far from its roots. He was a Christian feudal lord, not a Jarl or petty-king, and the men he commanded were soldiers rather than part-time warriors.

of alliances and dynasties that would eventually lead to a clash of armies in England and the end of the Viking Age.

The Normans

Rollo's acceptance of land in Normandy resulted in some important changes. By the time they had run their course, Rollo's Vikings would have become Normans, famous for fighting on horseback rather than on foot. But first they had to survive. Other Viking enclaves were established in northern Europe but no lasting dynasties emerged.

Rollo's people were forced to undergo a period of social evolution, from the fairly loose system used by the Vikings into something more Frankish. The Vikings were used to a system of 'loyalty freely given', whereby a leader was in charge because his followers wanted him to be. Authority was a two-way street and followers could transfer their loyalty elsewhere if they were displeased. As they became Normans, Rollo's people moved to a more formal system whereby those in power had a right to be, and their followers had strictly defined duties.

By the time this change was complete the Normans would be the instrument of change, bringing about the end of the Viking Age with their invasion of 1066 AD. In the meantime, Rollo's fledgling post-Viking state would have to struggle through many challenges. His son William was known as 'William Longsword', which does not imply a peaceful rule.

RIGHT: By the time of the 1066 invasion of England, the main Norman striking arm was armoured cavalry, with infantry and archers in a supporting role.

He died by assassination in 942 AD, but by that time he had expanded his father's realm by a combination of warfare and diplomacy.

William's illegitimate son Richard 'The Fearless' ruled until 996 AD, reuniting his realm after it was divided upon his father's death. King Louis IV imprisoned the young Richard and seized his lands but was defeated by Richard and his allies, who restored Normandy to the rule of Rollo's dynasty by 947 AD. Thereafter, Richard made good alliances and strengthened his realm, creating the powerful state that would launch the 1066 invasion of England.

Richard II of Normandy continued this trend, forging an alliance with the King of France and, later, with England. His sister Emma married Aethelred II of England, giving the dynasty a claim to the English throne. He died in 1026 AD and was briefly succeeded by his son, Richard III, whose sudden death put his brother Robert on the throne. Robert was involved in international affairs and considered an invasion of England. He died while on pilgrimage to the Holy Land in 1035 AD, leaving his young son William as his heir. William II of Normandy was illegitimate and was known as William the Bastard until his successful invasion of England. Thereafter, he became rather better known to history as William the Conqueror.

ABOVE: **William Longsword was a successful ruler who knew when to use his sword, and when not to. His death almost spelled the end for the fledgling Norman state.**

Trouble in Jorvik

While Normandy was evolving from a Viking conquest into a feudal realm the Viking kingdom in Jorvik suffered difficult times. King Aethelstan, grandson of Alfred the Great, conquered York and defeated Viking attempts to retake it. His conquest of the last Viking kingdom in England gained him the title of King of the English. His relations with King Harald Fine-Hair of Norway were good, and he fostered Harald's youngest son Haakon.

ABOVE: **Amlaib Cuaran is also at times known as Olaf Sygtryggsson or Olaf Cuaran. He was a quintessential Viking adventurer who managed to gain and lose a throne on four or perhaps even five occasions.**

Hearing of Harald Fine-Hair's death, Aethelstan gave Haakon the ships and men he needed to campaign against his brother Eric Bloodaxe, Harald's successor. Haakon drove Eric from Norway and took his place as king, while Eric fled to the Orkneys and then to Jorvik. There, in 947 AD, he was proclaimed king. The events leading to this are somewhat unclear, but it seems that Northumbria had broken away from the English throne and had been more or less independent since Aethelstan's death in 939 AD.

Olaf Guthfrithson restored Viking rule to Jorvik. His father had ruled both York and Dublin, and died in 941 AD. His successor was Olaf Sygtryggsson, also known as Amlaib Cuaran, whose career reflects the fortunes of the Vikings in the British Isles at the time. Amlaib Cuaran gained and lost both the thrones of Jorvik and Dublin on at least two occasions.

The Viking position in York was weak and shaky in 947 AD, and Eric Bloodaxe was just the sort of strongman who could cement Viking independence in northern England. His reign was short, however. During 947 AD, Eric Bloodaxe had to confront a shipwrecked Egil, his old enemy. Egil bought his life with a poem in praise of Eric, who forgave Egil the killing of his kin and absolved him of blood-price before freeing him. This gesture may seem unduly generous, given the bad blood between the two, but Egil gave Eric a priceless gift with his epic poem – the immortality of word-fame.

It was just as well for Eric Bloodaxe that he gained immortality when he did, for in 948 AD he was deposed. The English, under their new King Eadred, launched an attack that did great damage and threatened worse to come. This distinctly Viking approach succeeded: the Northumbrians decided to dethrone Eric Bloodaxe.

Eric's replacement was Olaf Sygtryggsson, also known as Amlaib Cuiran, who had returned from Ireland for another brief stint on the throne at York. He may have had the favour of the English king as he was the godson of Edmund, Eadred's immediate predecessor. However, Eric Bloodaxe returned to the throne in circumstances that remain unclear. It is known that the Scots raided into Northumbria at this time, but exactly who fought whom is a matter for conjecture.

It seems that Eric emerged victorious or at least managed to grab the throne, but two years later, in 954 AD, he was deposed a second time. He met his death in battle at Stainmore, probably in a last stand against overwhelmingly powerful pursuers.

Afterwards, Jorvik was very much a possession of the English throne for several decades. England remained strong under a series of effective rulers and was able to deter or beat off raids without being unduly threatened. Invasion was out of the question, and there were no Viking kingdoms remaining within England.

Aethelred 'the Unready'

However, in 978 AD Aethelred came to the throne as a 10-year-old boy. He would become known as 'the Unready', a name derived from *rede-less*, which translates as no-counsel, or 'poorly advised'. By 980 AD Viking raiding parties were harrying the English coast on a small scale, which grew over time.

In 991 AD, Olaf Tryggvasson attacked the English coast with 93 ships. He was met at Maldon by a force under Ealdorman Byrthnoth and during the initial standoff Olaf offered simply to go away in return for a bribe. Byrthnoth declined and offered battle, successfully holding the end of the causeway along which the Vikings had to move to reach the mainland.

The Vikings broke this excellent defensive position by the brilliant stratagem of asking Byrthnoth to move back a bit. This was phrased as a challenge to Byrthnoth's honour, essentially asking him to fight fair. He sportingly pulled his troops back, allowing the Vikings to move across the causeway from the island where they had landed, and a 'fair fight' – in which the Vikings outnumbered the English militia – then ensued.

BELOW: Byrthnoth's stand against the Vikings won him word-fame but also resulted in his death. A more pragmatic approach to the battle might have resulted in prosaic victory.

Byrthnoth was mortally wounded and many of his men fled, but his personal guard fought to the last around his body. The Vikings probably admired this courage and might well have been impressed at the poem composed in Byrthnoth's honour by one of his retainers, but they were no doubt more pleased with the relatively easy victory that misplaced chivalry had won them.

In the event, the heroics of the Battle of Maldon made no real difference. With the Vikings abroad in numbers, Aethelred the Unready offered Olaf Tryggvasson a large bribe in return for not harassing English shipping or raiding the mainland. This may have been the first time that payments to the Vikings in return for peace were referred to as Danegeld, but the term has been retroactively applied to all such payments in the Viking era.

Increasing amounts of Danegeld were paid in the next few years, allowing Olaf Tryggvasson to increase his power and the level of threat he posed. Aethelred tried to break the cycle by attacking the Viking fleet, but his plans were betrayed and once more he had to resort to throwing money at the Vikings in return for a brief period of peace.

In 994 AD, matters grew worse for England as Olay Tryggvasson joined forces with Svein Forkbeard, King of Denmark. A series of savage but not always successful raids compelled Aethelred to hand over yet more cash, which had the effect of getting rid of Olaf Tryggvasson for good. He was converted to Christianity in 994 AD, with Aethelred as his sponsor, after which he sailed to Norway with much of his force.

The Danegeld extorted from England was the foundation of Olaf's bid for the Norwegian throne. He was successful and founded the city of Trondheim in 997 AD as an easily defensible seat of government. From there, he set about consolidating his rule and converting his kingdom

BELOW: **The payment of Danegeld was an act of submission that helped the Vikings grow stronger and their victims weaker. This ensured that the cycle was not broken, as the victims were spending too much on bribing the Vikings to prepare properly for defence.**

to Christianity. This was not an easy process and often involved torture or forcible conversion, which made Olaf many enemies. He is credited with baptizing Leif Eriksson and thereby helping spread Christianity to the western edges of the Viking world.

Olaf's reign ended in 1000 AD when he was defeated in a sea battle in the Baltic, off the island of Svolder. Despite having the largest and most powerful ship in the Viking world, the famous *Long-Serpent*, Olaf's force was massively outnumbered and his 11 ships were defeated. He is recorded as fighting until his flagship was about to be taken, then leaping overboard. Although there were wild tales of his survival, Olaf never re-emerged onto the world stage and his kingdom passed under Danish control.

ABOVE: Olaf Tryggvasson rammed Christianity down his subjects' throats at sword point; an effective and very Viking way to go about spreading religion.

A Worsening Situation

In the meantime, things just got worse for Aethelred and England. Svein Forkbeard of Denmark continued to extort ever-greater sums from England, and the periods of peace they bought were far too short. Aethelred tried to improve his position by a marriage alliance with Normandy, but this produced no real

ABOVE: **The capture of the Archbishop of Canterbury was a sharp indication of English weakness. Subsequent events actually improved things for the English by causing some former raiders to defect to the defenders' side.**

improvement in the situation. Aethelred's problems were compounded by treachery within England, and much of this was blamed – rightly or not – on Danish settlers living on English soil.

On St Brice's day in November 1002 AD, Aethelred's forces launched a massacre of Danish settlers. The attack was timed carefully – it was Saturday, traditionally the day when Vikings bathed and washed their clothes. English women who had married Danes were not spared, and nor were their children. Among those killed in the attack were kin of Danish King Svein Forkbeard. Inevitably, the raids became more damaging, as did the price to halt them for a time.

The English response was confused and ineffective. The *Anglo-Saxon Chronicle* laments that Danegeld was offered too late each time, after the worst of the raids, and that military forces were always in the wrong places. Policies were formulated but not carried through, and the Vikings raided at will.

During this period, probably in 1010 AD, Olaf Haraldsson (later King Olaf II of Norway), is credited with using grappling hooks and vigorous rowing to pull down the fortified bridge defending London. The practice of fortifying bridges to impede Viking progress had been in use for some time, so it is possible that the incident occurred. However, it is hard to find any evidence beyond the nursery rhyme 'London Bridge is Falling Down'.

In 1011 AD the Vikings took the Archbishop of Canterbury hostage, which should have been a brilliant and lucrative masterstroke. However, despite the payment of a massive ransom, his captors somehow managed to kill him in a drunken brawl. There was a time when murdering eminent Christian clergymen was just a day at the office for Viking raiders, but at that late date in the Viking era it was too much. The event caused some Vikings to switch sides and start fighting to defend England.

Despite the contribution from outraged Viking warriors, England was tottering. In 1013 AD, Svein Forkbeard launched an invasion. The Northumbrians came over to his side, but London repelled an assault. Undaunted, Svein and his son Knut overran Wessex and Mercia, while Aethelred fled to Normandy. Svein Forkbeard held England for just five weeks before his death in early 1014 AD. This left the young Knut in charge, and he decided to pull back to Denmark for a time. The following year, Knut launched a renewed invasion of England, to which Aethelred had returned, and in 1016 AD was marching to meet the English king in battle at London when news came that Aethelred had died.

> 'BE NOT A BRAGGART FOR IF ANY WORK DONE BE PRAISE-WORTHY, OTHERS WILL SING YOUR PRAISES FOR YOU.'

King Knut

Knut, or Canute, earned the nickname 'The Great', yet he is recalled for rather optimistically ordering the tide not to come in and being disappointed. This is deeply ironic, as Knut did indeed order the tide not to come in, and it did indeed ignore him, but he fully expected it to. What is rarely recalled is that he then proclaimed to his subjects that the authority of kings is nothing compared to that of God, who rules the universe. He is said never to have worn a crown after this date.

Whether or not the incident actually happened, it is notable that it revolves around a Viking king proclaiming his insignificance in the face of the Almighty. Knut's pagan ancestors, who would insult, berate and even threaten their gods for not doing as they wished, might have found this attitude a little strange, but in truth the Vikings of Knut's time were very different from their predecessors.

Knut brought renewed prosperity to England, not least because he did not have to collect vast sums of money to buy off the Vikings. With the assistance of the church he was able to unify the kingdom to some degree. After generations of conflict between Anglo-Saxons and Vikings, a new brotherhood was not going to appear overnight, but Knut managed to forge some bonds between his disparate people.

It is perhaps a measure of how successful Knut was that little has been recorded about his reign. Raids, battles and outrages make the history books; years of peace rarely do. Little of note seems to have happened in England in Knut's reign, which was probably a welcome change for those under his rule.

In 1019 AD, Knut's brother Harald died. He had ascended to the Danish throne when Svein Forkbeard died and his death made Knut king of both Denmark and England. Meanwhile, Olaf Haraldsson, possibly the destroyer of London Bridge, had driven the Danes from Norway and was ruling there as Olaf II.

Olaf had been on the Norwegian throne for as long as Knut had held England, but in 1028 AD Knut invaded and drove out Olaf with the aid of many Norwegian nobles. Olaf, who had alienated many of his important subjects, was driven into exile in Kievan Rus. Two years later he attempted to retake his throne but was again defeated.

Knut was now king of Norway, Denmark and England.

BELOW: **Knut the Great proclaims the insignificance of men in the face of God, an act of Christian piety that might well have scandalized his ancestors.**

The task proved too great and around 1035 AD, Magnus the Good, illegitimate son of Olaf II, drove out Knut's regents. Knut's death in 1035 AD created a confused situation in which his son Harthacnut inherited the throne of Denmark and later that of England. He lost Norway to Magnus Olafsson, or Magnus the Good, who was later crowned King of Denmark upon Harthacnut's death in 1042 AD.

The Final Act

Harthacnut's death marked the end of Danish rule in England. The throne went to Edward, son of Aethelred, who became known as Edward the

The Empire of
Knut the Great

Knut's Empire

Knut's Vassal states

States allied to Knut

Norway
to Knut 1028–35

SWEDEN

Local
Kingdoms

DENMARK

Irish
Kingdoms

England
to Knut 1016–35

POLAND

Normandy

LEFT: **King Knut
inherited widely
separated lands, and it
was perhaps inevitable
that he did not manage
to keep all of them in
the face of opportunistic
adventurism on the part
of other claimants.**

Confessor. His reign was mostly a stable and successful one,
but royal power was eroded somewhat. Edward died in 1066 AD
without clearly naming an heir. This created the circumstances
under which the final act of the Viking Age was played out.

There were various claimants to the throne of England.
Duke William of Normandy had a claim by way of the marriage
between Aethelred the Unready and Emma of Normandy. The
English nobility convened and chose Harold Godwinson as
their king, crowning him on 6 January 1066 AD. According to
some Norman sources, Harold had sworn to support William of
Normandy in his claim to the throne, and, if so, then this was
obviously a breach of that promise. This claim may have been an
invention on the part of William of Normandy. He was at first
unable to find much support for his bid, but when the story came
out that Harold Godwinson had broken a promise sworn on holy
relics, the wind changed. Support came in and William began
constructing his invasion fleet. This was one of many occasions
when a leader of Viking origin used the church for his own ends.

ABOVE: **Harold Godwinson's coronation as King of England may have been a breach of a promise made to William of Normandy. William claimed it was and launched an invasion to take the throne for himself.**

Harold Godwinson was also of Viking descent. His father, Godwin, was a mercenary and raider who had settled in England. During the chaotic rule of Aethelred the Unready, Godwin extended his power until he controlled much of the region. He assisted Edward the Confessor in ascending to the throne, acting as kingmaker, but ended up in dispute with the king due to Godwin's favouritism towards his Norman kin and friends.

Godwin was exiled as a result of this dispute, but was so powerful that he was able to return and more or less demand to be reinstated. Godwin's son Harold continued his father's work, and may have been sent to the continent in 1064 AD to discuss succession issues with William of Normandy on behalf of the English king. If so, this was when the infamous promise was made.

The Last True Viking King

Harold Godwinson moved his forces to the Isle of Wight to meet the invasion, but by September it had not come, so he pulled back to London. In the meantime, however, a different threat was emerging. Harald Hardrada was half-brother to Olaf II of Norway, and had spent many years in exile as a result of conflicts between the Viking kingdoms. During this time he commanded the Varangian Guard and also spent some time as a mercenary and raider. The funds he amassed during this time supported his bid for the Norwegian throne.

In 1042 AD, Harald Hardrada left Byzantine service and began preparations for his campaign. Allying with the opponents of Magnus the Good, Harald demonstrated his intent by raiding in the Baltic during 1046 AD and was invited by Magnus to co-rule Norway. Magnus had not wanted conflict with Harald, and when he died the following year Harald became sole king. His rule was harsh, hence his name Hardrada, meaning 'stern counsel' or simply 'hard ruler'. However, his reign was stable and prosperous.

> 'WHEN MEN MEET FOES IN FIGHT, BETTER IS STOUT HEART THAN SHARP SWORD.'

Harald of Norway made war on Denmark throughout most of his reign, attempting to take the Danish throne. He finally renounced that claim in 1064 AD, but was invited in 1066 AD to become king of England. The invitation came from Tostig Godwinson, brother to Harold Godwinson, who agreed to fight alongside Harald in his bid. With support, finances and a blood claim, Harald had a good chance at seizing the English throne and, in September 1066, he landed in northeastern England.

Harald's forces numbered about 9000 men and 300 ships. They ravaged the eastern coast and sailed up the Humber, heading for York. English forces met them at Fulford and a battle developed. Initially the English were successful, striking as the Vikings were still deploying. However, a redeployment of reserves and additional Viking forces arriving late to the battle turned the tide and the English were heavily defeated. Casualties on both sides were serious, but the battle broke the military strength of Mercia and Northumbria.

York agreed to surrender without a fight on condition that it would not be looted, and as usual in such matters a hostage exchange was agreed. The Vikings made camp at Stamford Bridge while the surrender of York was completed. It was there that Harold Godwinson's forces attacked. Hearing that his local forces, charged with repelling the invasion, had been defeated,

The Vikings Attempt to Seize the English Throne – The Battle of Stamford Bridge
25 September 1066

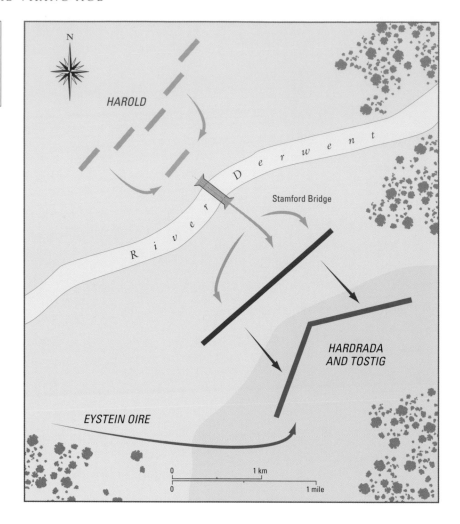

RIGHT: **Harald Hardrada's army was surprised at Stamford Bridge by the rapid response of the hard-marching English under Harold Godwinson. Harald's death turned a doubtful battle into a decisive defeat for the Vikings.**

Harold marched rapidly from London and arrived long before the Vikings expected him. As Harald's Viking force hurried to don armour and assemble its ranks, the English army closed rapidly. Their progress was impeded by the need to cross the River Derwent at a narrow bridge, which according to legend was defended by a lone but very large and energetic axeman who bought time for his comrades with a stand worthy of a place in the sagas.

Given a little time to prepare, the Vikings put up a good fight. The issue was in doubt for much of the battle until an arrow to the throat killed Harald Hardrada. He had been rushing ahead of his men, hewing down foes with his axe, and was within sight of victory when he fell. Thus died the man who might be considered the last true Viking king.

The battle was not yet over, however. As Harold Godwinson's men steadily wore down the Viking army, reinforcements arrived from the ships. They were too late to make any difference, and when it was all over there were only enough Vikings left to fill 24 ships out of more than 300.

William of Normandy Sets Sail

Two days after the battle of Stamford Bridge, William of Normandy set sail for England. He landed with about 10,000 men and got ashore without opposition. He was observed though; messages were sent, possibly by signal fire, and soon Harold Godwinson knew of the invasion. Having defeated Harald Hardrada and seen no signs of Norman invasion for months, it is possible that Harold may have felt secure in his position of king. If so, this new challenge in his hour of victory must have been a harsh blow. Nevertheless, he reacted decisively.

Having marched north from London to Yorkshire, Harold's army now turned around and marched back again. Pausing briefly in London to raise all the troops he could muster, Harold pushed on quickly. Perhaps he should have rested his army or raised more men, but there were sound strategic reasons for his haste. The location of William's army was known, and Harold did not want to have to chase his foes or look for them.

LEFT: The Viking army might have been overwhelmed sooner but for the heroic stand of a lone axeman. According to some legends he was slain by the spear of a man who floated under the bridge in half a barrel.

Besides, the land around the Normans' landing-site near Hastings was a natural bottleneck, offering the English a chance to contain the intruders. If William's army could be trapped, it might run out of supplies and be forced to withdraw or be worn down by a winter spent at the end of a supply line that ran across the notoriously stormy English Channel.

On 14 October 1066 AD, Harold Godwinson drew up his army on the Senlac Ridge. His force showed clear Viking influences. It included armoured axemen fighting in a style not dissimilar to that of the Vikings so recently defeated, backed up by a shieldwall of spearmen. The Normans had moved away from the traditional Viking system of warfare and had three specialized types of troops. Archers were used en masse to shoot holes in the enemy line, through which the elite of the army, chainmail-armoured cavalry equipped with lances and long swords, could smash a path. The infantry, meanwhile, would engage the enemy line in conventional hand-to-hand combat.

The Battle of Hastings

Harald Hardrada and his force had represented 'true' Vikings, but both the English and Norman forces were also of Viking stock. With the Vikings already out of the contest, the Battle of Hastings would now decide which of the successors got to write the history books. The English army had the advantage of a defensive position atop Senlac Ridge, and could afford to fight a defensive battle. If Harold Godwinson could avoid defeat, the status quo was to his advantage. This was just as well, since his force was at a disadvantage against the mobile Norman cavalry and the long-ranged archers. The Normans, on the other hand, needed a victory and thus they had to attack.

The English line held firm throughout much of the day, despite infantry assaults, cavalry charges and a constant rain of arrows. At one point the Norman cavalry fell back in apparent disorder and the shieldwall finally broke ranks to pursue. It is understandable that discipline failed in this way; tormented all day by archers, and hit at will by cavalry, Harold's English

'WHO CAN SAY WHAT SORROW SEEMINGLY CAREFREE FOLK BEAR TO THEIR LIFE'S END.'

warriors wanted vengeance. It was not a wise move, however. Once the wall was broken, Norman cavalry were able to smash the English units.

It has been claimed that the retreat of the Norman cavalry was deliberate, to draw out the English. However, the feigned retreat is perhaps the hardest of battlefield manoeuvres to perform, and almost all historical examples have been later shown to be a real retreat that unintentionally led to favourable circumstances.

Harold and his men battled on until the king was finally slain. The Bayeux Tapestry, a 'history book' written by the Norman victors and therefore biased in their favour, shows Harold hit in the eye by an arrow and hacked down by a Norman warrior. Which actually occurred is academic. With Harold dead and casualties mounting, the English army finally broke.

Victory at Hastings in 1066 AD enabled William of Normandy – William the Conqueror – to take the crown of England. This was the last occasion upon which England was successfully invaded, and it was a post-Viking state that accomplished it. The nearest thing remaining to 'true Vikings' was beaten at Stamford Bridge by Englishmen who fought in a similar style. Much can be read into the fact that the overall winners belonged to a post-Viking 'successor state', but William's victory was made possible by the Viking invasion in the north.

Would William of Normandy have taken the English crown without Harald Hardrada's unintentional assistance? Much speculation is possible, but the fact is that the Normans did win, and they cemented their control over the country to create a new state. The last of the Vikings had fallen, and their age was over but for a few postscripts here and there.

ABOVE: **Harold Godwinson may have been killed by an arrow or a Norman's sword. Either way, just as at Stamford Bridge, the death of the army leader spelled disaster for his force.**

10

THE LEGACY OF THE VIKINGS

The end of the Viking Age is an arbitrary determination imposed by historians to assist understanding of the complex tapestry of history. To those living in Norway or Iceland, the defeat of Harald Hardrada may have been significant but it was probably not considered the end of an era. Life went on as it always had.

Europe and Russia gradually adopted the feudal system that arose from the Viking attacks, and from it came the Medieval era, which led in turn to the Renaissance and eventually to the modern world. At what point did the Vikings stop influencing history? In truth, they never did.

The Vikings believed that word-fame lasted for ever, and through it a man could earn immortality. Some Vikings indeed did so: Egil and Eric Bloodaxe, Harald Hardrada and Harald Fine-Fair. The men who stormed Lindisfarne monastery in 793 AD are unknown to us, but their deeds are not. But there is more to it even than that. What the Vikings did shaped the world

OPPOSITE: The old alongside the new—Leif Erikson gazes at a far horizon outside the dramatic Hallgrimskirkja Church in Reykjavik, Iceland.

around them, for good and for ill. The cities they founded, the poems they left behind and the social values they lived by, which continued to be passed down long after the 'Viking Age' had ended, all influenced the development of Europe and Russia, and even left a tiny imprint upon the Americas.

Through the Looking Glass

Some influences are misunderstood or horribly distorted by the looking glass of later societies. The original Valkyries, for example, may have been elderly priestesses who put condemned men and captives to a gruesome death; hags rather the beautiful warrior-maidens depicted by nineteenth-century romantic artists. Vikings got winged helmets from the same source – an attempt to make them look more 'classical' in an era very taken with classical Greece and Rome.

Some words have been misused for so long that the original meanings are lost. Were *berserkers* a warrior tribe that was feared for their ferocity? Bare-chested psychopaths who went mad in battle? Or were they elite warriors who simply fought bravely and with disregard for injury? We cannot be sure. Even the spellings of words are confusing, coming to us through various dialects and written runic languages.

BELOW: **William the Conqueror enters London. The Norman conquest of England marked the end of the Viking Age and the beginning of a new era.**

LEFT: A Viking burial site. History has forgotten or distorted much of what the Vikings were and did, but even though its creators are long dead and buried the Viking legacy lives on to this day.

In truth, we will never know the whole story of the people popularly known as the Vikings, but we do know that they would not have referred to themselves as such. They were Norsemen, Danes, Icelanders, Greenlanders, Rus, men of Grimnir's warband, kin of Ingrod the Old… and, generally, they would be simply 'us'. And to some extent they still are. The world we live in today was shaped by many influences. Nations can trace their origins or elements of their history to Viking influences, and those nations influenced others. Great religious changes were wrought in Viking lands, and this too touched people in far-off regions that never saw a longship or a raiding party.

The Vikings were not the only major influence of the period, and others came before and after. But they were, without any doubt, a major part of the process that shaped the modern Western world and therefore the whole of modern society. A thousand years after the end of the Viking Age, their influence is still felt. Although not quite the same as explicit word-fame, that is a legacy of which they could rightly be proud.

INDEX

UK£14.99